PEN,
PAPER
&
PRINTING INK

by

Andrew King

WESTERN PRODUCER PRAIRIE BOOKS—1970

Printed and bound in Canada by
MODERN PRESS, SASKATOON

Dedicated to the memory of my wife
MABEL STIRLING
and my two sons
STIRLING
the better writer
and
WILLIAM (BILL)
the better printer

CONTENTS

PREFACE

A major but often neglected part of Canada's social and cultural past involves the history of printing and publishing. In this country, as well as in Europe, not enough has been said about printers and presses and their influence on our daily lives. One of the main reasons for this lack of emphasis on the art of printing is the very paucity of evidence. The historian is handicapped because such archives as manuscripts, proofs, account books and even the final productions, whether they be ephemera or elephant folios, have slipped away into oblivion.

Publishers, printers, typefounders, engravers, and their colleagues, from the birth of printing in Europe, to present day Canada, have often simply been too busy making a living to preserve records and to put down in writing the details of their work and their impressions of the world around them. Wars, fires, droughts and economic depressions have conspired to harass the printer. He has often been on the run—just to survive. External forces have been the major cause of the gaps in our printing past.

But there are some areas about which we are fortunate enough to know a great deal. There have been important exceptions amongst the publishing houses and printers, often those institutions and men who were the most fully occupied, but who had the tenacity and ability to pursue their craft and art and write about it. Such a man is Andrew King—publisher, printer, engraver—man among men.

Although the full story of printing in Canada has yet to be written there is no lack of colourful and rich material. It is replete with energetic imaginative and talented men and women whose continuing pioneer printing endeavours are around us everywhere. Three names dominate the scene because of their inventiveness, dedication and sheer talent— Evans, Dair and King.

It was James Evans, the Norway House missionary, who in mid-nineteenth century Manitoba, three hundred miles north of Winnipeg, invented the Cree syllabic symbols, cast his own type, and in some miraculous way managed to turn out books on birchbark. There was Carl Dair, the internationally famous type designer, printer and humanitarian, who shortly before his untimely death, finished the design of the typeface *Cartier*. Dair's *Cartier* was his gift to the nation in 1967 and it was the first text type designed in Canada by a Canadian. The third name is Andrew King, whose autobiography constitutes an impressive contribution to our printing heritage.

It was Carl Dair, who first told me something of the remarkable story of Andrew King of King Show Print. King's inventive genius, his steady application to printing and publishing, as well as his humane qualities, have long been known and appreciated by his friends and colleagues in

Canada. In recognition of his considerable creative talent there has been included in the recently established Bibliography Room for Graduate Studies at Massey College in the University of Toronto, a permanent place for the work of Andrew King, already well known as "King's Corner." On either side of his portrait are displayed several treasured examples of his large wood engravings. Andrew King shares this room with students at work on the subject of the history of printing and publishing.

Andrew King has always been a pioneer as the very appearance of this book will attest. It is, I believe, his engraving and the printing of three-colour circus posters in the nineteen twenties, thirties and forties which mark him as an artist and a major figure in Western Canadian and North American printing history. He began his engraving work in 1914, when, in his own words, "there was no one to teach it." Andrew King taught himself the art of wood engraving. Through the frustrations of trial and error, sometimes referred to as experience, he mastered his craft and went on to make King Show Print famous in the field of poster art. It was King Show Print of Estevan, Saskatchewan.

Pen, Paper and Printing Ink is an invaluable contribution to this country's social history. Pen, paper and ink are the ingredients but it takes a man to make them work. Andrew King did just that.

DOUGLAS LOCHHEAD,
Librarian, Massey College,
Professor of English,
University of Toronto.

Bibliography Room,
Massey College.

9 November, 1970.

Chapter 1

IN RETROSPECT

The first cold winds of early winter sent low-hanging clouds scudding across the sky, grinding the scattered snowflakes into white powder that whirled and eddied over the bare streets of the little western prairie town.

It was a dismal night.

The town's human inhabitants had responded to the dictates of nature's mood.

They had closed their shops, their offices and havens of leisure and retired to their homes, boarding houses, scantily-furnished rooms and shacks to seek whatever comfort their quarters provided.

Not a single pedestrian was to be seen, if anyone was looking, along the dark, deserted streets.

Even the homeless, hungry, foraging dogs had tucked themselves away in hidden corners where they could spend the night most comfortably.

One by one the house lights blinked out.

The entire town assumed the appearance of a place no longer inhabited by human beings.

There was a quietness that was accentuated by the eerie sound of the wind as it swirled and whirled around the silent buildings.

Yet, there was one evidence of living activity in all of the loneliness of the midnight hour that few would have noticed even though many may have known of its existence.

Rays of light came from two windows, well hidden in a narrow passageway between two buildings but a few feet apart.

Those gleams, weak, yet so incompatible with the entire

dismal scene and its timing, came from inside a little frame structure designed in a most frugal manner, reflecting the financial condition of the owners.

Built of lumber, one storey high, its front was painted. Its sides were not. A common, wooden, four-panel door and an upright, four-pane window did little to brighten its frontal appearance. The door gave entrance to a small room, with bare wooden floor and unpainted walls. It was quite evident this was an office. Here again frugality had dictated the furnishings, which consisted of one chair, one table cluttered with newspapers, and a home-made standing desk with sloping top.

A door in a partition led to a slightly larger room referred to as the workshop, though why it was so definitely defined and so isolated was a good question. Certainly the little front room was also a workshop, even though its product was different.

In the rear room were again to be found bare floors and unpainted walls with printer's ink stains here and there, fading into the overall smudginess resulting from air pollution common to all interiors in those years.

This building was the home of the town's weekly newspaper and printing office.

Crowded into the back room shop were two printing type case stands, a type cabinet with cases of different type, one imposing stone, a treadle job printing press, and a small newspaper press, the latter a simple machine which could only be operated by strong human muscles.

In the corner was an upended wooden apple box on which sat a small wash-basin and on the floor beside it a water pail with dipper. There was good reason to place the water pail on the floor—there it was closest to the refrigerative powers of the outside atmosphere.

In a central spot stood a cast iron, pot-bellied stove with a tin smoke-pipe connected by a complicated combination of vertical and horizontal pieces to a brick chimney. The latter was a little bit of luxury agreed upon as a wise fire-safety measure. The stretch of smoke-pipe insured maximum economic use of the heat produced by the fuel.

Three small coal oil lamps, with little handles for convenience in moving them to places where their dim lights might be temporarily required to lighten the gloominess of more remote corners, were set in wall brackets to which some inventive genius had added a minor improvement evidencing the continuing interest in betterment of still imperfect things that man had slowly developed over the centuries. The lamp brackets could be swung in a small arc enabling the precious light to be concentrated upon the area where it was most needed.

Two lamps illuminated the type cases on the top of the stands. In front of each was a man. Both were setting type in brooding, concentrated silence—silent other than for the click of the individual pieces of small metal type being dropped into the steel composing sticks and the unnoticed but ever present tick-tock of the wall clock as it registered the slow passing of minutes.

A new printer's apprentice, unfamiliar with the requirements of the trade, could only watch these two printers and hope by observation to gain some little familiarity with the techniques he knew he would need to acquire.

Otherwise, he added fuel to the grates of the pot-bellied stove as the temperature in the room dropped to uncomfortably lower levels.

Only occasionally were a few words spoken between the men—perhaps a query over some poorly-written copy, which has historically plagued compositors, or how much more work had to be done.

Midnight was passed, then, one o'clock in the morning and finally all the news copy had been set in type, sufficient to fill the waiting empty spaces in the newspaper pages. Proofs were taken of the type and this initial printing was carefully scanned for errors and these corrected.

Finally the set-up type was arranged properly in the page forms, spaced out to uniform tightness, squeezed still tighter by sliding wedges within a steel frame.

The two printers were intent on their work until the forms were lifted to the bed of the press. By then the time had passed when vocal interruption might result in typographical error.

"Well, that's that," said one to signify that the period of greatest work strain, and its accompanying silence, had ended.

It was three o'clock in the morning when the first copy of the newspaper was printed, but an hour's labor had still to be performed before the issue of 250 copies would be completed. The folding and the writing of subscribers' names and addresses on them was part of the next day's labor.

The end of the long day had arrived—a day that had begun at 8 a.m. the day before, for a total of 18 hours.

The final nine hours had been a steady grind without a recess—no coffee break, no lunch, with only an occasional drink of water from the dipper as refreshment.

So at four o'clock in the morning each one rolled down his shirt sleeves, donned coat and overcoat with collar turned up over ears. They blew out the oil lamps and struck off for home through the dismal night. They knew they had only four hours in which to get some sleep and breakfast before beginning the labors of a new day.

It was all a memorable introduction to the printing and newspaper business for the young country lad who, as a raw apprentice, had joined the little staff of the small town western (Manitoba) weekly that very day.

4

Chapter 2

CHILDHOOD DAYS

I was born in the year 1885. That year recorded the climax of the Louis Riel rebellion. These two events could not be considered of equal importance. Certainly they had nothing in common.

But it is always of interest to observe how unrelated occurrences will span distances and even the passing of years to sway the course of human lives.

The full import of the rebellion has become obscure to those living today. Some may never have heard of it. Those who have acquired some acquaintanceship with it through schooling or books can be excused for considering the uprising and subsequent related battles as a minor event because of the comparatively few hundred regular soldiers, militiamen, Metis and Indian warriors involved.

Yet the rebellion's ending brought more than a deep sigh of relief to those administering Canada's internal affairs and specifically so to those who carried the heavier and more intimate responsibility of supervising and shaping the growth of the economic life of the immense prairie west.

For Riel's activities had kept alive a threat of political dissension carrying with it a fear which held in check increased occupancy of the rich virgin land by hundreds who hesitated to go beyond the fringes of then existing settlements.

It was the defeat and capture of Riel which brought a completely new outlook and future promise to the vast prairies. There was land to be had for the asking plus a contract with the government requiring a term of residence of three years coupled with a stipulation that a minimum

5

number of acres of the quarter section applied for be broken and cultivated during that period of time.

Never had men 21 years of age and over of that generation been given such an opportunity to acquire land at such small cost. The ambition and desire to own it, to be master of their own earnings created by their own labors caused a surge of homesteaders to sweep over the prairies to settle in areas many days journey away from the only railway line that cut across the province of Manitoba and the North-West Territories on its way to the tidewaters of the Pacific Ocean.

Here was an opportunity to acquire independence denied them by the peasant conditions of the old lands from which many of them came. Each settled on the land still available which suited them the best. The conversion of prairie sod into productive fields began. It was the forefront of a new era in the history of the Canadian west. The hunters, trappers and traders were being pushed aside.

My father, who, as well as my mother, was born in Scotland, had come to Canada to carry on his vocation of building contractor. He had never worked on a farm. He knew absolutely nothing about the proper care of farm animals, or how to harness a horse, or hold a plow. Yet he succumbed to the excitement of the times and finally located a homestead about 12 miles southeast of Souris, Manitoba, which was then a little hamlet named Plum Creek.

Riel's downfall was the event which suddenly channelled his life into an unfamiliar vocation—something he had never dreamed of entering when he came to Canada—yet one in which he was most successful.

And I am sure that both he and mother were even happier in the thought of bringing up their family in the quiet countryside—once they became adjusted to the new manner of living—where in addition to work to be done there was time to think calmly, to discuss kindly and intimately the affairs of their neighbors, with occasional excursions into the events taking place in the old and new world.

There is no reason to suggest that, because I was born in the rebellion year that I was other than an average everyday sort of infant whose early days are filled with only an unconsciousness of all happenings but which vacuity, as time goes on, is finally disturbed by bits and pieces of everyday events which begin to create, stimulate and enlarge the wonderful human faculty, commonly designated as memory.

The nearest railroad to father's homestead was thirty miles away at Brandon, Manitoba from which point, building materials for a house, food, furniture, clothing, a plow and harrow along with a few other necessities were transported on several trips by wagon. The latter was pulled by horses over roads that were merely trails which no one needed to follow if they could find a better and easier route. These turned and twisted to follow the higher and dryer levels of prairie to avoid any chance of getting bogged down in depressions made soft by summer rains. With luck a one-way trip could be made in about seven hours.

Quite often two or three neighbors would make the trip together. Such concentration of manpower made it less hazardous.

The strange and unexpected, with even a touch of humour, could happen on occasion. When a neighboring Scottish homesteader was moving his first load of effects from Brandon he found that his wagon box was crammed so full and piled so high that there was no safe place left for a jar of "mountain dew" which in those days was justified as being a necessity for medicinal purposes in the remote countryside. At least such explanation had a ring of sincerity in times when doctors were few and far away.

The whiskey jars at that time were really of the kind seen in the modern movies and TV shows of frontier days. The crude container was merely a utility. It had no sales appeal with its rough exterior, a short neck and a convenient little handle through which a finger could be slipped for lifting or carrying it. It was the contents which created sales.

To leave the "gray-beard", as the Scots called it, would never do. Neither could the homesteader afford to leave behind even the smallest article of the well-packed load. But urgent need will find a solution to most problems. He slipped a piece of rope through the jar's handle and tied it to the reach of the wagon which is that piece of timber or metal below the

7

box connecting the front and back axles. Here, he was certain it could swing freely and safely as the wagon moved along the trail.

But when he reached his homestead he was "sair disappointed". Somewhere on the trail the wagon had passed over a stone high enough to strike the jar. All that remained of the jar and contents was the little handle and a bit of the neck.

It was in the late eighties when father moved his family to the homestead. Curiously enough my first conscious memory was that of seeing him on the roof of the house he had built, laying the last few bricks of a chimney. That brick chimney was a luxury in the eyes of nearby neighbors, who used tin pipes poking through a hole in the roof or a wall to carry away the smoke from their stoves.

The scenic background of the building is still a vivid memory—a monotony of level prairie with not a tree in sight.

The first day of school created the next flash of memory. What I learned that day I cannot remember in detail—maybe a letter or two of the alphabet. It was not too long until words such as "cat" and "bat" became easily recognizable and still later came the more tantilizing problems involving figures that had to be added, subtracted along with division and multiplication tables.

In those days the little prairie school house was considered more important than a church building, even by those who were intensely loyal to the conviction that man's chief end was to glorify God. Church services could still be held in school houses, or in homes or in the lea of some homesteader's shanty.

Classes usually began in April and ended in early October. It was too difficult to keep attendance up during the winter months, for the conveyance of children, sometimes up to three miles or better, was too uncertain because of snow, blizzards and lack of horse power. Even the cost of heating the building was a deterrent factor in the times when cash was scarce.

The curriculum taught was a simple one. There was time for little more than "reading, 'riting and 'rithmetic," with geography and a bit of history thrown in. When a few years later the subject of physiology was introduced some thought the educational planners had become too bold with an immodest subject.

But if a broad base was lacking, the subjects taught were firmly implanted by devoted teachers. The number of pupils attending any one school might be no more than a dozen. Rarely were there more than two to a class. This meant that every pupil received personal instruction. Grades were not clearly defined. When one book was mastered another one was begun even if it was in mid-term.

Somehow this somewhat irrational method achieved results. That little old school house—an experience no doubt matched at others—with about six to seven months' instruction each year, produced from one generation a healthy crop of graduates including a college principal, a prominent lawyer, a medical doctor and a civil engineer. The grounding they received carried the majority of them through university with honors.

Organized recreation was never thought of. The children took care of that themselves in games involving running and physical activity during recess periods to dissipate the energy which accumulated during the hours of study.

In retrospect, comparing it all with the multiplicity of subjects taught today, from simple spelling to modern mathematics and languages with a medley of others in between, plus organized sports, musical groups, debating groups, students' councils and whatnot, the schooling of pioneer days seems too simple and inadequate.

Yet somehow it worked. It was from the little old red—or white—school house of the rural parts that came a relatively large ratio of men and women who in due time rose to high levels in the business and professional life of the nation.

Chapter 3

PIONEER PRINTING

A history of the weekly newspapers of the Canadian west must begin with a recording of the circumstances which brought about their beginnings. Naturally, weekly newspapers at all times have required a minimum density of population to warrant their establishment, but the conditions existing in the pioneer days were unique when compared with those of later years.

Today, it could be the discovery of a new rich mineral area, or the setting up of a new industry some distance from existing centers of population, that provides a new opening for a newspaper. Instances such as these can be found in all parts of Canada.

How different were pioneer conditions. There were few people who had any more money than that required for current needs. Industry in any form was almost totally nonexistent.

The small villages and towns scattered here and there owed their existence entirely to the labors of homesteaders and incoming farmers who were fortunate enough to have a few dollars with which to make a down payment on a bit of land.

These were the men who first of all began to develop the broad rich acres of the prairies, in Manitoba and less rapidly in parts of what was then the North-West Territories. It was their labor and frugality coupled with their need of supply centers that started the little villages; into these new raw settlements moved the weekly newspaper publishers.

Some began with uncertainty as to their future; some with enthusiasm; many with dedication to provide what

leadership they could in public affairs; a few with fixed political allegiance that was reflected in their writings. In the main
they were printers first and writers last. Practice and experience provided the training for their careers as journalists
and businessmen. Not all were successful in a financial or
professional way, yet the marvel is that so many did succeed
in the face of the rigorous conditions which prevailed.

In the final analysis it was the homesteader who produced the monetary support of all the business transacted
in every little urban community. It was the direct support
in the manner of yearly subscriptions by the rural dwellers
that provided the basis on which all weekly newspapers
functioned. Merchants and others considered advertising as
a sort of perfunctory thing which could even be used as an
excuse for subsidizing a newspaper.

The pioneer homesteaders have all too often been considered as men that were physically strong, though with
bowed shoulders, gnarled hands, crude in their manners,
uneducated and completely lacking in culture—a list of characteristics seemingly in tune with the rigors of a harsh, un-
developed country with material shortages, economic handicaps, physical hardships and challenges.

There were those who conformed to such a description,
but these in the struggle to improve their daily needs and
economic resources also strove to fulfill visions of a fuller,
more soulful and finer social future for their children.

There were examples of culture plentifully sprinkled
across the countryside, enriched by those who, by chance or
decision, came from countries across the seas where they had
been raised amid social refinements, intellectual and artistic
background in their native lands.

There were those who could discuss with knowledge and
authority the essence and message of classical literature and
art. There were those of the gentler sex who could produce
the atmosphere of a drawing room in a scantily furnished
interior of a small prairie home. There were those whose
skill on a musical instrument brought pleasure to others on
a dance floor, delight and inspiration through concert music
and added deeper reverence to religious service.

There were men and women with fine voices whose renditions of the old songs with tuneful music and poetic and revealing lyrics never grew tiresome—so different from the present day fad of distorting good singing voices into gasps, whispers, moans and glissandos while endeavoring to give feeling to lyrics that have no message.

It was unfortunate that not all of these people with varied artistic talents did not make a success of their farm efforts, but the memories they left brought rich reward to community life.

The early settlers were avid readers of their local weekly newspapers. These at first were comparatively small in size with five columns to a page, and often no more than four pages. As the number of papers increased a firm in Winnipeg began the production of "ready-prints."

These were sheets of paper printed on one side and were supplied in one-, two- and four-page sizes, the latter being the one most generally used with the home town publisher printing four pages.

The ready-print pages always carried a romantic fiction story in installments which always broke off at a most exciting or dramatic moment, leaving the reader eager to scan the next installment. Another continuing feature was the International Sunday School lesson.

Because of their varied appeal, these features were considered subscription list builders or at least retainers.

The ready-prints were also flooded with patent medicine advertisements considerably lacking in good taste both in text and appearance.

In the main, they provided bulk to the weekly newspaper as well as adding to the local coverage a bit of national and world news and articles of general information.

The printing equipment of all the early weekly newspapers was barely adequate to produce the weekly issue and the small amount of commercial printing used by local businessmen, mainly letterheads, envelopes and statement forms.

Usually there was little more than enough type to set all the news required to fill out the pages. The larger size type for advertisements was a motley array of styles. It was only in the '90s that type designers began to turn away from the ornamental letters with shadings and curlicues, and produce more legible and forceful styles.

This revolution in typography appeared at the same time as a completely new concept of advertising—specifically that of newspaper advertising—which was stimulated on the American continent through the study and initiation of more aggressive methods in merchandising based on greater emphasis on sales.

But until the fanciful and bizarre styles of type were completely replaced by the newer simpler styles, all country printing offices used both, resulting in typography that was little less than hideous when compared with modern standards.

The presses used were mostly hand operated and of simple design. Some newspapers were printed on platen presses, one page at a time. These were put in motion by the use of a treadle with the operator standing on one leg and treadling with the other.

As a matter of fact, muscle played an important part in the printing trade in those early days.

Gutenberg, the father of printing, after the passing of five centuries would have found himself quite at home in the country newspaper office with equipment little improved from that which he used.

Type was still set by hand in the same manner as it was in his day and printed in most cases on the very same kind of press as used by the earliest printers. About the only up-dating touch given these newspaper presses was a new name attached to them when American manufacturers put them on the market.

They were then called Washington hand presses. The tugging of a lever required to print a sheet of paper called for a technique of its own if one were to reduce the muscular stress to the least tiring minimum.

The most important of all improvements to the mechanical process of printing was the invention of the inking roller both in the formula of its rubber-like composition and its cylindrical shape which invested it with continuity of revolving motion and providing it with greater coverage.

Previously all type forms were inked by daubers. These were round-bottomed leather bags tightly stuffed with cotton or other fibre into the shape of a flattened ball with the upper portion fashioned into a handle.

With one of these in each hand, the operator would smear some ink on the flattened ends which were rubbed together until the ink was evenly spread on their surfaces. The type form was then inked by daubing it before each sheet of paper was printed—a very slow process indeed.

With the advance in engineering skills bringing about the assembly of cylinder, gears, cams, rollers and rotating parts, the cylinder press was invented—a machine to which power could be applied with greater speed of operation.

Granted, there were cylinder presses in the larger cities in Canada during the 1880s that were driven by steam engines, but for the pioneer weekly newspapers on the prairies such an installation was too cumbersone to transport across the long trails and too costly to buy and operate because of the small income received by the publishers.

It was only when the stationery internal combustion engine (the gasoline engine) became available that the country printing offices began to eliminate the muscular drudgery required in producing newspapers and commercial job print-ing. With this convenient source of power it became possible to employ typesetting machines and power presses to keep pace with business expansion brought about by increasing population and larger rural income.

But even in the face of tremendous strides in all phases of science producing inventions undreamed of over a century previously and the uncovering of new fields of research among nature's elements, it should not be overlooked that there were men, thorough in their studies, mainly concerned in the formulas of materials used in printing, whose final decisions have come down practically unchanged over a span of five centuries.

At a time when chemistry was in its most primitive form, the chemists of those days decided upon a formula for type metal which has never been improved upon other than a slight change of proportions of the constituents which in the main were made necessary by its use in typesetting and casting machines requiring an ever present supply of molten metal heated to a high degree of temperature.

This amalgam of three metals, either used in typesetting machines which cast solid lines of type or in the casting of single letters is made up of lead, tin and antimony. Sometimes a little copper is added in making type for hand setting.

Old specimens of printing also reveal the perfection in the making of printing inks. These early craftsmen made black inks that are just as black today as the day the printing was done.

So at the turn of the century the average equipment in the country newspaper office in regard to machinery was a hand operated old style newspaper press, a platen press for job printing and a small paper cutter—the minimum equipment with which the shop could operate.

It was into such a plant that the young country boy—as did dozens of others—went to "learn" the printing and newspaper business.

Like the basic form of earlier schooling, such an experience had its advantages. There was no specialization of work. One had to set type, make up forms and operate the presses. It was a time when inventive minds began to challenge the dormant state of the printing trade insofar as equipment and technical methods were concerned. New and improved machines were built. The study of typography was encouraged.

To be in on the early beginnings of this revolutionary movement provided an unusual opportunity to follow its gradual progress like a course of instruction—progress that still continues at an active pace through the designing of new automatic machines with ever increasing capacity both in speed and quality of work produced.

Chapter 4

APPRENTICESHIP

M any beliefs are held, all with a measure of support, as to the main influences during childhood which bring about the choice of vocation a boy or girl accepts in later years.

These beliefs include the influence of race, family life, surroundings, education, economic status, social contacts and immediate opportunity. It can be easily understood how each of these, or several combined, are capable of producing the motivations that lead young people to make the important decision.

At the time when settlement of the Canadian prairies began to expand and population increase, the environment did not provide much of a range of vocations from which a choice could be made.

There were trades demanding skills in the use of rudimentary tools such as blacksmithing, carpentry, masonry or tailoring. One could become a shoemaker, a painter, a plasterer, or a barber. In these trades, while they were not exactly glamorous, there was plenty of room for work expertly done.

There were no openings for women. It was unladylike for a young woman to take a position other than that of a "domestic." Secretaries in offices were males. When the first lady clerks appeared in retail stores many eyebrows were lifted.

There were many jobs for men requiring little more than strength to use a pick and shovel.

Science was still dragging its feet as it plodded towards breaking down the secrets holding clues to a vast new world of technological progress calling for profound knowledge and technical skill which later mushroomed into the immense field of specialized employment which exists today.

Looking backward, it can be readily understood how contact with and assessment of the comparatively scanty list of occupations played an important part in the decision of a lifetime: how any vocation promising something more enticing and exciting than the drab occupations so prevalent in those early years could easily become a youth's choice.

With true Scottish loyalty and patronage, father's bookshelves carried a complete set of Sir Walter Scott's Waverley novels and Chambers' 10-volume encyclopedia. In recognition of the talents of the great English writer, a full set of Charles Dickens' fiction were also there, along with other worthwhile books including the Works of Josephus (now a museum item) to make up a somewhat extensive library not usually found on most homesteads.

A mammoth bible lay on a center table. It contained some particularly beautiful lithographed biblical scenes so vivid in composition and coloring that repeated viewing did not lessen their fascination.

From the very first, the books interested me. Probably not so much as literature but in a physical sense. Wonder and enquiry followed as to how they were printed and bound and by what manner of means the beautiful gold lettering was stamped on their covers.

Maybe if those books had not been present another interest would have developed.

It followed that every bit of technical information available was collected and perused. With a pocket knife attempts were made to carve letters on the ends of little bits of wood to reproduce type. The results were no doubt atrocious but the experience brought familiarity with the correct formation of letters as used in printing. It was all good fun and in a sense rewarding.

Quite opportunely, when I had finished school, a local newspaper advertised for a boy to "learn printing." This was the customary form used at that time to invite applications for such positions. Apprenticeship was rarely, if ever, mentioned. That word, to people from the old lands, carried a connotation of servitude.

The Canadian west was a new land, already forming its own ideas and ideals relating to individual liberty and social freedom, parallel to and inspired by the wide open spaces of the vast prairie land as yet uncomplicated by population pressure.

Enquiry revealed that the job was open immediately and that for the first year compensation would be room and board at the editor's home. At that time the prevailing charge for such at regular boarding houses was $2.50 per week. The subject of increase in pay was to be given consideration at the end of the first year but it was implied that this might be as much as one dollar per week.

The advertisement by the newspaper was rather ineptly worded. It asked for an "intelligent" boy to learn printing.

When the somewhat timid young boy from the country arrived to begin his career, he was at once dubbed "Intelligence."

This did not make the atmosphere altogether pleasant but it made one fact quite clear—adjustment would have to be made to the ways of the new outside world.

One other fact became evident: A nickname to be freely used must be a short word, preferably with a specific tang. One syllable words are always most popular in the field of slang. The word "intelligence" had just too many syllables to slip easily from the tongue. It was too cumbersome.

The one on whom it was imposed was relieved to find it being replaced by the more friendly use of a contraction of his Christian name.

It just happened that the country boy began his duties on the day the weekly newspaper was to be printed. Because of the departure of the former apprentice, the staff was short-handed. It consisted then of two partners, owners of the business.

Typesetting of the news to fill the columns was much in arrears. By the time this had been completed, the forms made up and printing of the small edition was done, the hands of the clock indicated 4 a.m.

Nine additional hours had been put in during the night over the regular work hours. There was no payment for overtime, no coffee break, and no complaining. It was simply accepted as part of employment that the newspapers must be mailed by a certain hour no matter how much extra time was required.

Yet the little staff of three was back to work four hours later, ready to put in the regular day's contribution of nine hours. Fifty-four hours was presumed to constitute a full week's work.

Fortunately, the first night's experience was not repeated, though it was a rare occasion when some overtime was not worked, in order that the paper could be printed and mailed on time. After all, there were railway mail services that had to be "caught" and some of these ran only twice a week.

The newspaper was a typical weekly in a typical Manitoba town of around 700 population. The equipment was similar to that found in every country office—meagre, and though as modern as available in its class, it was wholly rudimentary.

Every letter, whether it was in news column or advertisements, had to be picked up individually and assembled by hand. Then after each issue had been printed all of these single letters had to be distributed back into their respective boxes of the type cases.

This work was the most time-consuming of all in "getting out" the weekly newspaper. The typesetter had to stand (or sit on a stool, which however, did not permit a slight swaying of the body so essential to rapid typesetting as the workman reached into the farthest away type compartments). Standing or sitting, he was positioned in front of a rack or stand upon which were set at suitable angles, one above the other, two type cases.

The upper case contained the capital letters, fractions and other miscellaneous characters. The lower contained the small letters, figures and some punctuation marks. It was from this arrangement that the common terms of "upper case" and "lower case" originated, designating capitals and small letters.

There was pride in becoming a speedy typesetter and

19

records were being continually striven for in the time required to set a "stickful" of news matter. A stickful amounted to a block about two inches wide by eighteen to twenty lines deep. Anyone setting a stickful in the commonly used size of news type in less than twenty minutes was rated a speedster. Some had records as low as sixteen minutes.

Typesetting machines of today whose keys, cams and pawls are operated by a perforated tape can produce fourteen lines or more per minute.

But the old slow pace had compensations. It developed the urge to set copy accurately. A word left out or a few letters missing brought on a lot of trouble in correcting the errors later.

There was more intimate training in the use of punctuation marks and the correct "style" in the use of capital letters, paragraphing, indentations and spacing, all of which are important in the proper arrangement of type particularly in advertisements and commercial printing.

This can be compared with the pleasing balance and detail in an artist's masterpiece, and places type composition in the field of art.

There were no typewriters in a country town in those days. Every word of copy placed before a printer, other than reprint copy, was written by hand. Incidentally, it was quite some time later that the use of typewriters in filling out legal forms in Manitoba was authorized.

All weekly newspapers carried little items of personal news from rural areas, usually designated by the name of its school district or in some cases the name of a little post office set up in a farm home, maybe ten or more miles from town, and which was a worthwhile convenience in the horse and buggy days.

Many of these contributions by rural correspondents required careful study of the distorted formation of individual letters, some knowledge of the circumstances creating an item, plus a hunch, in order to decipher with some degree of accuracy all that the scrawling was expected to convey.

On one occasion a contributor was finally rounded up and asked to unravel the mystery of his scribbled text which included some proper names. He peered and squinted and hummed and hawed.

Finally he gave up with an explanation that became something of a classic in newspaper circles. It was: "I never was no phrenologist at spelling."

It is significant that the newspapermen who, in the first ten to fifteen years of this century, followed the westward progress of railway construction, were nearly all graduates of country offices in Manitoba and Ontario.

Their training had covered a little more than that of the trade of printing. Their close contact with reporting (even though their duties had been confined to the "back office") had also prepared them in some degree for the assuming of the responsibilities of the "front office" with its emphasis on news writing of local happenings.

The acquiring of the little bit of knowledge required to do simple bookkeeping in the form of most rudimentary records was easily accomplished.

There were no records to keep of taxable or non-taxable sales; no income taxes to deduct from the payroll; no unemployment insurance stamps to calculate and purchase; no pension plan funds to remit; no statistical breakdowns to report to government agencies. With no personal income tax to pay there was not even an obligation to balance books or prepare an annual financial statement. It was all so simple. Newspapermen never had it so easy in this phase of their business operation.

In general, these were the conditions prevailing in country printing offices at the time the young farm boy moved into town to become the printer's devil.

The special duties allotted to him at first included the sweeping of the floors, lighting fires in the stoves every cold morning, together with the removal of ashes from same, carrying a pail of fresh water daily from the nearest well, the filling of oil lamps, together with wick trimming and globe cleaning, shovelling snow or sweeping litter from the front sidewalk, and miscellaneous errands.

But not all offices insisted that these simple household duties be carried out in meticulous fashion. Yet this was

but the beginning of a training leading into the fixing of tidy
and orderly habits that are so necessary in the successful
operation of a printing plant.

Weekly newspapermen are an independent bunch,
(thank goodness!) but unfortunately for us, we exist
in an age when failure to exert our full strength is costly.

—IRWIN McINTOSH, *North Battleford News
Optimist.*

Chapter 5

FIRST EMPLOYERS

The country boy found his two employers kind, considerate and willing to take extra pains to teach and give guidance to the extent their own experience allowed. Each had received only a partial vocational training. They approached every new problem in a rational manner, adding to their own knowledge in the progressive way so characteristic of those with serious desire to develop their skills.

The senior partner, Wm. J. Barclay, did the news writing but when occasion demanded could do a stint of typesetting with creditable speed. The other partner, Robert H. Cook, was the printer.

While their personalities differed they were both typical of Manitoba newspapermen of the first 25 years of this century. As did so many others, each developed talents which with the passing of years brought well-deserved prominence.

Deep in his heart Barclay had a love for adventure though his quiet and modest manner kept this trait well hidden.

He satisfied his yearning by launching a row-boat each summer on a different prairie river. His companion was Rev. J. S. Muldrew, Presbyterian minister at Souris.

Their journeys followed the courses over which Indians, early explorers and traders had paddled their canoes, enabling them to delve deeply into history created by the arrival of the whites, setting the precedent for today's "voyageurs" of which the late well-known journalist Blair Fraser was one.

Their meals were cooked on camp fires, their food supplies being augmented by the shooting of wild ducks, geese and prairie chicken. There were no closed seasons for game in those days.

The night's camp was set up in primitive fashion.

Their most noted and daring trip was down the North Saskatchewan river from North Battleford to the head of Lake Winnipeg. They passed through miles of countryside in which there was not a single human being, and where damage to their boat, loss of provisions by upset or accident to either one of them would have left them in a critical situation.

A year was spent in acquiring a knowledge of the river and the country it flowed through. Geophysical maps were studied to learn the location of rapids, the valley pattern and the course of the stream in detail, all invaluable in assuring safe travel and determining good landing and camping spots. Locations of widely separated trading posts were pinpointed; such information was vital should emergency arise.

The trip was fascinating and thrilling, for the Saskatchewan river had been the four-lane highway of the fur trade in the days of the North West Company and Hudson Bay Company, with memories still lingering over its entire course.

On its waters was started the long journey of the precious fur harvest to the hat makers of Britain and France, serving the beau monde of Europe.

Flowing into it were the many rivers which tapped lakes and smaller streams throughout the choice beaver country to the north.

Past these, and the many long-deserted sites of pioneer trading posts, rowed the two modern voyageurs on into northern Manitoba where the river became a tortured, twisting stream with divided channels whose destinations were hidden amid evergreen growth.

Then finally the quiet waters of Lake Winnipeg were reached. At Grand Rapids they took steamship passage to Winnipeg.

Barclay's stories of their experiences under sunshine, rain, hail, wind and chill, were given fitting prominence in the daily press.

Yet he omitted relating one experience which nearly

resulted in a terrible tragedy. Circling closely around a sharp point on the river they were suddenly greeted with the sight of a flock of ducks on the water. Barclay snatched up the loaded shot gun, took quick aim and fired. Only then did he realise that in his hasty aim the charge of shot passed only a few inches away from his companion's head. "I have never touched a gun since. It just proved that I cannot trust myself with one again," he told a few friends many years later.

Robert Cook was an alert, clean-cut man, active in church work and athletics. He had speed and agility on the lacrosse field—a game in which Souris held national recognition—and when playing soccer he could make the ball do tricks.

He became a member of the "Small-Town-Boy-Makes-Good Club" in later years. Selling his share of the business to his partner in 1901, he went to Arcola, Sask., then a dead-end on a new railway branch line and a booming town. There he engaged in the real estate and insurance business.

His analysis of the latter convinced him of the place and need of farm crop hail insurance based on certain concepts. He set up the Farmers' Mutual Hail Insurance Co. Under his management it proved so successful and expanded so rapidly that its head office was moved to Regina.

Shortly, the company's business reached such a volume that it became necessary to reinsure a goodly portion of the coverage.

Cook headed for London, England, to consult with Lloyds which at that time was the insurance centre of the world. He quickly placed all the contracts he desired.

At the same time he came under the scrutiny of the keen and alert brokers associated with that vast insurance empire, a scrutiny which resulted in 1935 in his appointment as broker for Lloyds in Toronto.

Thus did Cook graduate from a partnership in a small newspaper business housed in a little frame building to the ownership of a metropolitan insurance business with scores of employees in his own large office building in the heart of Ontario's capital.

Both Barclay and Cook were truly distinctive members of the early fraternity of weekly newspapermen in Manitoba.

The latter not only carved out for themselves many niches in local, provincial, and even national history, but trained a large percentage of the printers who later moved into Saskatchewan and Alberta to open up newspaper offices of their own.

There were such men as Walpole Murdoch (Hartney Star) noted nature writer and painter of prairie scenes; Jim Cowie (Carberry News-Express), who took on the exacting position of King's Printer; W. J. Udall (Boissevain Recorder), a human dynamo who practically founded the International Peace Garden in Turtle Mountain; Gordon McMorran (Souris Plaindealer), noted for his research on the trails of early explorers; Tom Beveridge (Melita New-Era), prominent for his vivid reporting of a series of bank robberies along the international border and on one occasion following the trail too closely to find himself challenging the robbers and himself receiving a bullet in the shoulder; Harry Munro (Swan River Star), who founded the first paper north of parallel 53 at The Pas; Bill Marsh (Dauphin Herald-Press), noted for his pungent editorial writing; Ira Stratton (Stonewall Argus), prominent in the political field; Ron Tuckwell (Pilot Mound Sentinel), with sports stories in leading magazines in Canada, the U.S. and Great Britain; Fred Beech (Glenboro Gazette), who trained scores of young people in the mastery of brass and reed instruments; Billy Rowe (Manitou Western Canadian), a lawyer-editorial writer of renown; William Stone (Rapid City Reporter), whose activity was successful in establishing soccer football as a major sport in Manitoba; Bill Hanks (St. James Leader), who quit the weekly ranks to become mayor of the City of St. James; Frank Manning (Reston Recorder), who graduated more top-notch all-around printers than any other news-paperman in the entire north-west; and many others leaving the impress of their personalities in a distinctive manner.

Between them, Barclay and Cook broke down the monotony which might easily have depressed their new apprentice through the unchanging routine of hand-setting type, printing the weekly issue and then distributing the type, letter by letter, back into the type cases ready to set up the news for the next issue. Or treadling the platen press during the last two days of the week after the newspaper work had been completed, to produce the odd order of job printing that was "on the hook."

This was an idiom commonly used when printer's copy was impaled on a curved spike hanging on the wall or type case stand.

The editor did all his writing as he stood in front of a high desk with a sloping top. The flat-top desk was still an innovation at that time. The sloping top was used everywhere—offices, business places and schools.

Mr. Barclay was unobtrusive and thoughtful to a degree, much different to the type of reporters pictured at times in movies.

To be a competent reporter and editor in those early years on a weekly newspaper—and even today when it is a one man job— such a person should have at least some degree of familiarity with a varied number of subjects. In a sense, he had to be a sort of super-specialist dealing with news stories based on grain growing, livestock, sports, politics, municipal affairs, building, markets, education, churches, weddings and pink teas.

Invariably, the degree of accuracy and style in which news stories were written was determined by the range of the writer's background of the subjects involved.

Only on rare occasions was Mr. Barclay's temper ever visibly ruffled. That is another sign of a good newspaperman.

At that time most of the large business institutions with branch offices across Canada had not adopted the policy of ordering their printing needs from one office convenient to their headquarters. Banks were no exception.

On one occasion the local branch of one bank placed an order for 1000 promissory note forms, which were promptly printed and delivered. A few days later Mr. Barclay was passing its entrance. It happened that the manager was standing there. With a miscalculated sense of humor he quipped, "Barclay, you are a very close counter. You sent us 1001 note forms."

The thought of his integrity being questioned, and a

lot of time being taken to count the forms, plus knowledge from experience that the bank never gave anything away, roused the Scottish ire of Barclay.

"You were only charged for one thousand so I want that extra one back" he quickly retorted; he stormed into the bank and would not leave until the manager handed it to him.

It was not unusual for banks, which for some time were permitted to issue their own bank notes for currency, to send shipments of such to local branches, printed four to a sheet. These lacked one signature on their face.

The bundle would be carried down main street from the bank to the printing office as casually as one would tote a bag of groceries.

It was a rare experience for everyone in the office to gather around the paper cutter while the bills were being cut apart. It was a thrill to gaze upon more thousands of dollars of paper money that they would ever dream of handling themselves.

It was the duty of the bank manager to sign his name on each bill to make it legal tender.

The theory of transporting new bank notes with a sig-nature lacking was that it would be of no value to anyone who might steal it in shipment. This was no doubt an echo of the wild bandit days in the United States.

But even the most illiterate thief could have easily penned a scrawl as indefinite and unreadable as the signature of the average bank manager, all of whom seemed to take delight in writing their name in a manner that looked like a piece of tangled thread.

Not everything that was done in the town was approved of personally by Mr. Barclay, but he left the discussion of public affairs to the people themselves to talk about and form their own opinions.

This decision to refrain from creating or emphasizing and division of opinion, and only reporting facts involved, no doubt had much to do in keeping the community free from personal bitterness to a marked degree.

At the same time, there were happenings which in part at least could have been turned into exciting stories had sensational journalism been practiced by this rational editor. No one will ever know how many of such a nature he hid deeply in his memory.

Like that of the bank teller who led the choir in one of the churches. One Sunday evening he sang in solo with his beautiful baritone voice "When I Shall Meet Him Face to Face." Monday morning he did not show up at the bank. Enquiry revealed that he had left town, someway for somewhere. Bank inspectors found a shortage of several thousand dollars in the cash under his care.

He was finally traced to the United States but at that time there was no extradition agreement with that country.

The pleasing sequel to the story was that a complete payment of the shortage was made later.

Another bizarre happening in the town remained a closely-kept secret in the printing office until it was finally spoken of by the few who knew of it, after all the participants had passed from life on this earth.

The highlight of the story was a duel fought by two well-known personages in the town.

The principal figures were a somewhat emotional male music teacher and a highly respected business man. The beginning of it all was the sudden infatuation of the teacher with the wife of the business man, who, while quite discreet, allowed herself to be flattered by the attention paid her. Whisperings began to spread through the community.

The music teacher's friends gave him good advice which he did not heed, blinded as he was by his infatuation.

One Sunday evening three of them dropped in on him in his suite in a casual manner as they had done often before. During the chatting which followed the music teacher was asked if he had seen so-and-so lately, naming the husband of the woman involved.

The question had barely been asked when the husband burst into the room, angry to the point of violence. He grabbed the teacher by the throat and began to choke him.

The others quickly separated them, calmed the husband down somewhat and in doing so emphasized that the use of violence of that nature was no way to settle differences they might have.

During the conversation which followed, a half humorous reference was made to the old practice of dueling. The suggestion appeared to capture the fancy of the two principals, both in a belligerent state of mind.

So a duel was finally agreed upon. Revolvers were to be the weapons and the encounter was scheduled for next morning at an early hour in a wooded portion of the town park. Seconds were chosen and a doctor was to be notified to be on hand.

At the appointed hour all were there. The combatants were placed back to back, instructed to take so many paces, turn around and fire their weapons. The sound of the shots came almost in unison. The husband fell, struggled a little, slumped, sighed and lay still. His second was hovering over him instantly. The teacher ran up to the fallen man, saw a red stain on his shirt, and with one look, fled the scene. He packed his belongings, which were few, hired a livery rig and left town never to return.

Blank cartridges had been used. The red stain was paint that had been hastily daubed on. It was all a well-planned farce, magnificently executed. It completely washed out the unpleasant situation.

Such were the sort of events which occasionally riffled the placid routine of small town life, but which never appeared in public print.

At the end of six months, the country boy, who had been receiving board and room, along with all the comforts and hospitality of Mr. Barclay's happy home, as compensation for his time and efforts in the printing office, was advised his rate of pay would be increased by 50 cents per week, cash money.

This made it possible to purchase a new pair of trousers on terms of 50 cents down and 50 cents every two weeks. More recent years have no claim to originality of credit buying. The only change in the plan is that now one must sign documents.

While this added income would appear almost as nothing today it then had a purchasing power of significance. Bread sold at five cents a loaf; eggs were eight cents a dozen, butter 12 cents a pound.

One day Mr. Barclay opened the following conversation:

"Andy, what do you want to do after you learn the trade? Do you want to work for someone else or own a business?"

"Well, Mr. Barclay I would like to own a business."

"Fine, and what kind of business?"

"One like this one of yours, Mr. Barclay. A weekly newspaper and job printing business. I think I would be quite happy with that."

The right flavor of his final remark can only be properly expressed by reproducing his Scottish accent: "Aye, Andy, I ken what ye are thinkin'. Ye can see the money comin' in but ye dinna see it gaein' oot."

In later years this sage remark was often recalled with full appreciation of a viewpoint commonly held by those unacquainted with the economics of the operation of any type of business.

It is an expression of a hard fact that most weekly newspapermen became intimate with as they pursued their vocation in the small towns and villages on the prairies.

Chapter 6

WORK AND PLAY

An apprentice to any trade soon finds out that he must use the language peculiar to it. This, in most cases, has been acquired over the passing of centuries though the use of nouns and verbs with meanings entirely different from those common to the English language and with the spelling of such words unchanged.

The result is a lingo distinctive to each vocation. To be properly understood by any tradesman, communication with him must be in the words of the language he is accustomed to use.

It is probably not at all strange that new words were not derived throughout the years to replace those used in various trades which already had a number of different meanings—something that has always made the English language confusing and difficult to learn by those whose native tongue is one of the many others used throughout the world.

The printing trade has a "jargon" all of its own. Possibly it is one of the greatest offenders in its use of words in such a way that they have no relationship with their original meanings. Yet modern dictionaries will, in respect to the varied use of such words, include their vocational meaning among the other definitions, but unless one is a painstaking student of Webster's classic text-book their multiple manner of use can become perplexing.

Take the word "chase", for example. One's first thought is to associate the word with the pursuit of something. Used in the printing trade it is very much different from that. Then it becomes the name of a rectangular steel frame into which assembled type or plates are placed for printing.

The type so assembled is termed a "form" which in everyday usage refers to an athlete's physical condition or the wondrous shape of a bathing beauty or artist's model.

A form is squeezed tightly inside a chase by the use of "quoins" which from the sound of its pronunciation suggests metallic money. Instead, they are wedge-shaped pieces of steel which would be most uncomfortable to carry around in one's pocket.

The use of quoins in tightening the type form inside the chase so that it can be safely moved intact from place to place, is known as "locking up" which has nothing to do with locking doors or securing criminals in prison cells.

The first printing of a type form is known as a "proof" which has much in common with the use of the word in relation to evidence, but certainly far removed from its reference to the strength of alcoholic drinks.

When a printer speaks of "impression" he refers to the amount of pressure applied to a type form when it is pressed against paper in the process of printing. It has no connection with a vague feeling or belief.

"Make-up" is a word used daily in every printing office but the work it designates has nothing to do with the use of powder, lipstick or other beauty aids, though it does play an important part in typographical beauty. It is the arrangement of type lines, large or small, such as appear on a newspaper page or a piece of commercial printing.

In making up a form the printer has to "justify" the type and spacing material he handles. This means that such has to be fitted together so that none of the pieces remain insecure. This is very much different from the usually accepted meaning of the word which is to vindicate or prove something is just.

"Plate" is the general term used to designate a stereotype or picture cut for printing, and not the target over which pitchers are expected to throw baseballs or the dish used in churches to take up collections.

"Furniture" in a printing office is the name given to pieces of wood or metal, of less height than type, which are placed around forms to fill up space not occupied by type forms inside a chase.

When forms are "put to bed" it means that they have been placed on the flat metal table of a press which moves back and forth under the revolving cylinder whereby a sheet is printed with each reversal of the bed.

"Slugs" are used in typesetting. Not the gastropods related to snails, but material usually one-twelfth of an inch in thickness and of required length between lines of type.

The word "ream" used as a verb to describe the enlarging of a hole through the use of a reamer becomes sheets of paper in printer's parlance.

"Quire", the word which designates 25 sheets of paper, is strangely enough also the alternative word for "choir," with similar sound of pronunciation. Incidentally, this fact was used by craft crooks in byegone days, who would frequent the writing rooms in hotels and by subtle conversation get others to bet with them that the name of a group of singers was not spelled q-u-i-r-e. The crooks always won the bet when reference to a standard dictionary proved that such was correct spelling.

Many other words such as type, reproduction, negative, padding, fountain, copy, feature and sentence used daily in the printing and newspaper trade have widely different meanings than those usually associated with them.

For the apprentice it was not too difficult to acquire the lingo applied to definite objects or their use. But it took more time to memorize and become familiar with the names of type sizes which were still used by printers up till the close of the 19th century. By that time the use of figures to designate type body sizes was taking over. This was the American point system and is now used throughout the world. It is based on the lineal measure of one inch which represents 72 points.

There were no schools of printing but there were printing trade journals with excellent articles which made them almost standard text books. These were most timely and helpful in both the fields of typography and mechanics, for the trade had begun to discard the shackles which had kept it static for many years.

Most apprentices read and studied these articles assiduously and sought to apply such newly acquired knowledge whenever possible. All this was basic to the growth in craftsmanship and technical skills sprouting at the time and which still continues at an unabated pace half a century later.

Because of this, the many country newspaper offices became the major training ground and source of supply of personnel to satisfy the needs of commercial and newspaper offices in the cities.

In retrospect, it becomes, quite evident that any boy connected with a weekly newspaper office had the privilege of a wider contact with, and knowledge of, all the activities in a community than those in any other type of employment.

Certainly he had opportunity to become familiar with personalities in the community, how they lived, their relationships, what they accomplished, their motives; whether they were rich or poor, old or young, political aspirants or less ambitious persons. Life in a small town was an open book which could be scrutinized at will with enlightenment for those who desired it.

But the employment of spare time was a 'teenagers own responsibility. Rarely was there any organized effort to provide athletic or recreation facilities for either boys or girls.

Unoccupied land (if there was any) would become a village green. Its appropriation for use as a playground was an accepted custom. The owner rarely objected.

There were no dance halls, public libraries, picture shows, restaurants or ice cream parlors in which to loiter (there were only poolrooms) and with no place to go, very little dating between boys and girls.

There were no automobiles to race; no radio or television. School buildings were only class rooms. No one thought of smashing windows, toting guns, taking drugs, or defying the police.

There was the occasional house party, skating in a rink (if there was one) or on a pond or river; church services morning and evening with Sunday school in the afternoon.

If one were so inclined, there might be lacrosse or hockey to play, but each had to buy his own equipment and more often than not pay a share of expenses when playing a game at a neighboring town. Expenses would include the hiring of democrats drawn by horses, from the livery stable.

Of course, some boys would steal a few carrots from someone's garden and on Hallowe'en push over a few outhouses and at the cost of much physical effort put wagons and buggies on the ridges of barn roofs, but there was no continuing threat of harm to persons or property, no gang disturbances or riotous lawlessness, no strikes for special rights at schools or colleges.

Yet young folk did not whine at being ignored, or having little to do, or no place to go in their spare time.

There was only one public hall in Souris which carried the imposing title of Sowden's Opera House, even though not one opera company had ever graced its boards.

It had a semi-circle of private boxes in a balcony which were rented to the elite on a yearly basis and in which they appeared in evening gowns and swallowtails on auspicious occasions, such as the annual visits of Harold Nelson's Shakespearian Company.

Nelson was a drama and elocution teacher in Toronto and chose his most talented pupils for his group. Among them was Clifford Lane Bruce whose name eventually appeared in lights on Broadway, New York, and Billy Yule who achieved a high rating in comedy roles in later years.

Nelson would play three nights in Souris with a change of bill each night, a somewhat heavy task for one leading tragedian. "Hamlet" was one of his favorites and with an attempt at greater reality in the grave digging scene a fair sized hole would be cut in the centre of the stage floor.

As the curtain rose on the scene the first grave digger would be discovered half hidden in the hole from which he would slowly shovel dribs and drabs of black soil the while carrying on the philosophical conversation with grave digger number two, in the words dictated by the immortal Shakespeare.

The appearance of a musical company with a chorus

line was not greeted with this circle of formal dress. Its advance agent had slyly whispered, here and there, that it was a burlesque show. All the seats in the hall were occupied by males but the show did not measure up to their expectations.

The most daring part of the show was when the stage curtain was slowly raised revealing first the bare feet, then the ankles and finally the knees of the chorus line. At that point the curtain was suddenly dropped.

In the comedy field was Harry Lindley and his players who would stay for a week putting on a different play each night. There was "vaudeville between the acts," performed usually by singers of popular ballads of the prevailing sentimental type such as "On the Banks of the Wabash Far Away." or "Take Me Back to Ole Virginny." Admission for children was 10 cents, adults 25 cents.

Andrew McPhee, who incidently was a prairie boy brought up near Wolseley, Sask., moved his company in a special railway car playing one night stands. While playing in the summer time he often used a tent in which to put on his show.

Every man in his company "doubled in brass" so that on his arrival in town his band would parade down the principal streets with its strident notes splitting the air waves out beyond the town's perimeter. The seasons he played "Uncle Tom's Cabin," the one bloodhound, so necessary in suggesting the proper atmosphere of the famous book, would be a main attraction in the parade.

McPhee eventually owned his own circus in the United States for many years, travelling under the title of Andrew Downie Circus.

The famous Richard & Pringle's Minstrels, one of the finest groups ever, played Souris occasionally on fill-in dates. After hearing its band on parade and in evening pre-show concert, few could resist the urge to attend the show.

The street parade was one of the most colorful features of the entertainment business around the turn of the century. It was, in fact, the "come-on" for the main show.

Quite naturally, the half-mile long circus extravaganza

was the most spectacular. A circus in those days travelled on its own special train and would arrive in each town at an early hour in the morning. Its parade was always held before the noon hour and was a free attraction which drew into town the rural people from miles around.

Sleek prancing horses in teams of two, four and six pulled the gilded chariots, band wagons, wild animal cages with a variety of critters from monkeys to hippopotami. There were acrobatic floats and, of course, a noisy, wheezing steam calliope, now rarely seen outside a museum or a private collection of antiques.

With rollicking, roving clowns it was a moving show of many features, the spirit of which has never been duplicated completely, even by the imaginative and ornate Grey Cup and Rose Bowl parades.

The noon band concert usually sponsored by theatrical groups, was quite naturally less exciting than the circus parade, but then "everyone loves a band" and in those days bands were not plentiful on the prairies. A smartly turned out band with a drum major, playing stirring march tunes at quickstep tempo caused hearts to beat faster and immediate cares to disappear. The echoes of some of these great tunes still remain in the memories of those whose lifetime extends back far enough.

The Kickapoo Indian Medicine Show was one of several of that type to play Manitoba towns. Admission to it was free and the first half of the show would be vaudeville. This was followed by a medicine talker whose lingo dealing with the symptoms of many illnesses caused people to doubt whether they were as healthy as they always thought they were. Many eagerly purchased the so-called Indian elixers, mainly alcohol, at one dollar a bottle and salves that were little better than axle grease.

Then there were the Musical Eckhardts, advertised as the Swiss Bell Ringers, with octaves of bells, each perfect in pitch, rung in harmony that was most pleasing. They also performed on glasses tuned to different notes by the varying amount of water poured into each. Music was produced from these by drawing the palms of their hands, on which pumice had been rubbed, across the tops of the glasses. These and other unusual musical effects made them a most popular attraction.

Remembered among the more talented artists would be Jessie Maclachan, the famous Scottish soprano, and J. W. Bengough, Toronto Globe cartoonist, with a rapid-fire, bright monologue of general comment illustrated by sketches rapidly drawn and including likenesses of well-known local people whose faces and characteristics he had memorized during the afternoon as he strolled along the business streets.

All this variety of entertainment brought a bit of the brightness of the far-away land of make-believe to young and old alike in the isolated towns of the west, and was doubly welcomed by staffs of all weekly newspaper offices. It was the privilege of the press to be given complimentary tickets of admission in abundance.

There had always been music in our family home on the farm. Father had a fine tenor voice and mother had quite a good soprano voice; both had choir and chorus experience in Scotland. A pedal organ was one of the first luxuries brought into the house, and after a few elementary lessons graciously given by a neighbor lady, three of my brothers began to play with a fair degree of skill. One took up violin as well, and though in the main self-taught, in later years he played in symphony orchestras in Vancouver. Number two of the trio became quite a passable 'cello player.

Unrecognized at the time, the ever-present sound of music from voice or instrument created a latent bent of which I was not aware until I left home.

It was little wonder then, when concert, dramatic and professional entertainment companies of great variety played in Souris, that I became increasingly attracted by show business in general.

Not that I wished to become a performer of any kind but I did become an appreciative "fan," just as later in time, in the heydey of motion pictures, millions of people on this continent followed the ups and downs of the picture industry and their favorite screen stars with intense ardor.

Undoubtedly this somewhat superficial acquaintanceship

with the mechanics of show business, its language, mannerisms, successes, failures, actors, actresses and performers of all types became of considerable value to me in later years when first seeking to sell a service to show companies, impressarios, circus and carnival owners.

To be able to converse in the language of any profession breaks down the unseen barrier so often present between its sophisticates and those of the outside world.

Souris in one instance was fortunate in having a young man, Charlie Cook, who introduced an activity that was most unusual at that time. He gathered together about twenty 'teenage boys and organized them into a brass band. He gave them all good basic instruction and the organization held together for some years, until the departure of too many of its members caused it to fall apart.

This was broadening experience and several of the members in later years added to their incomes by playing in dance orchestras and bands in larger centers.

Another of the rewards from the short musical experience was the ease with which almost any instrumentalist could get a position. There were many small brass bands in prairie towns and villages and it was not unusual to see numerous advertisements in daily newspapers asking for bandsmen. Oddly enough, the positions open were mainly for printers and barbers. Maybe these were the tradesmen who moved around the most!

Election campaigns periodically added a special spice to the lives of adults as well as 'teenagers of the male sex. Women were not considered intelligent enough to have a part in politics. They had no vote.

To most male adults the issues of the day were serious matters. To the 'teenagers the public meetings provided stirring entertainment.

Those were the days when Sir Clifford Sifton, Hon. Thomas Greenway and Hugh John Macdonald, son of the great father of confederation, drew overflow crowds wherever they spoke. Meetings were tumultuous; there were bursts of cheering, applause and spontaneous response to quick wit on the part of a speaker when challenged by a heckler in the crowd. Forcible ejection of the latter sometimes added to the excitement.

On election nights crowds would gather in public halls to hear the returns through messages carried by juvenile runners from railway telegraph offices. Those anticipating a win for their party would occupy the front row of seats until maybe disappointing returns leading up to a defeat would cause them one or two at a time to slink into the background or leave the hall, while the supporters of the winning party would gradually move forward to take over the vacated chairs and respond boisterously to each favorable report.

The pulsating atmosphere of those special hours have almost entirely disappeared as folk sit in their own homes and listen to election returns through radio or TV. The conflict of exhilaration and disappointment on the part of the audience on such evenings created an emotional scene rarely witnessed in modern times.

The names Clifford Sifton and Thomas Greenway are seldom mentioned today but the pages of history record the manner in which they shook the Canadian west out of its lethargy and in a short space of years set it on a course that finally made it one of the main supports of the Canadian economy.

Sifton's well-planned and forceful immigration policy placed thousands of new families on the vacant lands of the three prairie provinces. Immigrants were carefully selected and located on the type of land best suited to their capabilities. Greenway, in a less spectacular manner impressed the farmers for the first time with the need and value of a better type of livestock, including in his program the importation of top quality purebred sires from overseas.

Whether they realized it or not, the 'teenagers of those years had a stake and future in this economic upsurge. It carried on its crest thousands of new business openings, creating a field that for almost half a century saw the highest infiltration of weekly newspapers known in all time.

Chapter 7

BROADENING EXPERIENCES

Though the mass inflow of new settlers was mainly in Saskatchewan and Alberta, which at that time were still districts of the North West Territories, the province of Manitoba indirectly benefited a great deal. The upsurge was felt everywhere.

It was a time when every business was stimulated by the infiltration of new capital.

It was also the time which marked the first encroachment of the mechanical and scientific age, with all its impatience and future promise, the impact of which definitely began to change the entire economic and social structure of life on the western plains.

A few of the more quickly-adopted items which reduced physical stress and provided new services may be noted here. One of these was two- or three-furrow gang plows with spring seats on which the rider could sit all day, guide his team of horses and control the operation of the machine by adjusting levers within easy reach. This early attempt at automation did away with most of the fatigue previously brought on by walking behind a single furrow plow, steered by the operator as he grasped two long handles, the while endeavoring to keep his motive power—two horses—pulling the plow ahead in the straightest line possible.

New types of harrows and disc plows with greater capacity and efficiency came on the market. Binders, or reapers, were constantly being improved. Threshing machines were out-fitted with self feeders, grain baggers and blowers to shoot the threshed straw into large piles away from the machine, thus doing away with the old method of "bucking" the straw by horses away from the head of the elevating carrier before the pile got high enough to clog it.

The steam traction engine also came on the scene to become the first travelling mechanical power to reach the farm. No longer were horses needed to draw the threshing machine from one site to another.

The horse as motive power on the farm was on its way out.

The lady of the house was not forgotten by inventors. Old rub-a-dub-dub washboards, on which the family wash was laboriously scrubbed clean, were replaced by wooden slatted contraptions doing the rubbing through rotating motion of the simple mechanism propelled by human arms, all a great time- and muscle-saver.

Bicycles were becoming common, mostly with young folk. For the reason that no lady would think of wearing slacks (that name was unknown then) a specially designed frame enabled women to ride these bicycles with every-day, full-length skirts.

The first telephones were being installed in towns and villages where demand warranted.

Concrete paving was beginning to replace plank sidewalks, though streets were still to remain unpaved for years.

In Souris, an acetylene gas plant was constructed to provide street, business and household lighting. The coal oil lamp was being replaced. The use of electrical current was still in its infancy, and confined to large cities.

Souris had become a railway divisional point which added several miles of switching tracks to the railway yards and new families to boost the population. A subdivision was added to the townsite to which a convenient approach was built in the form of a swinging bridge across the Souris river. The bridge is still in use and has become a tourist attraction, presenting a beautiful setting when viewed from upstream against a background of curving banks that divert the river's course into a graceful arc.

More houses were built. All businesses became more prosperous. New professional personnel moved in and began practice.

The staff of *The Souris Plaindealer* was increased by

three to become five. The space occupied by the plant was doubled.

A five horsepower gasoline engine was installed. It was one of the town's showpieces as a mechanical miracle—a fact no one will dispute. It marked the beginning of the intro-duction of internal combustion engines and what the latter did to the world when the inventor put it on wheels is now common knowledge.

Today few people realize what the stationary gasoline engine meant to the weekly newspaper publishers all over the west. It brought to them a type of power at a price they could afford to pay when electricity was not available, and with its flexibility, it fitted neatly into the efficient operation of a small plant.

The old "armstrong" press was thrown out of the *Plain-dealer* office and replaced by a large cylinder newspaper press. Power was transmitted from the engine to the press through a welter of belts and overhead shafting.

The small Gordon jobbing press which had been driven by leg power applied to a treadle was also "hooked up" bringing smiles to the faces of those who had operated it by standing on one leg and treadling with the other for hours at a stretch, the while using one hand to feed into the press and the other to remove from it the sheets of paper being printed. The word ambidextrous does not properly describe this feat performed by four human extremities simultaneously. Quadradextrous would be more fitting, though the dictionary does not contain such a word.

The newspaper was enlarged to six-column size. Adver-tising and subscriptions increased. The printing of farm auction sale posters became the one important line of job printing as farmers sold their farms and moved westward. The introductory wording on these posters followed a stereo-typed form reading "unreserved auction sale of horses, cattle, farm implements and household effects."

There was an unusual exception in the destination of one farmer. He was an Englishman who had made a rare financial success of his farming and at the same time had developed a great deal of aggressiveness and initiative.

He decided to return to his native land, taking with him the latest Canadian machinery and methods, rent acreage for a farm of a size unheard of there and, as he said, "show the English how to really farm the new way in their own country."

In this respect he displayed the instincts of a showman; this was also apparent in the type of sale posters he had printed for his auction. They were the largest ever issued for an auction sale and near the bottom carried one line in very large letters, reading "The Souris Brass Band Will Attend." A close scrutiny revealed the word "not" in quarter inch high type between "will" and "attend."

George Waldey's sale was an outstanding success, as were his later farming operations in England, where he was elated at having created a demonstration of a large operation causing a furore in British agricultural circles.

The country boy felt at this time he should move to broader fields for wider experience in the printing trade. On occasion he had been left in charge of the business while Mr. Barclay and his friend carried out their holiday hobby of travelling prairie rivers in a boat.

So into Winnipeg the boy went to meet his first disappointment. On making application to join the typographical union he was told he was not old enough, the minimum age required being 21 years, a figure arrived at no doubt by calculating that the age of 16 would be the youngest that a boy could graduate from high school plus five years of apprenticeship.

However, this first setback was soon taken care of on the union's initiative. An application was signed with the space for age left blank as the applicant refused to sign it with the figures 21 in the age space. No false statement was signed by him though it was quite apparent that a fictitious figure could be inserted later.

A rumour floating around later implied that there had been the possibility of a strike coming up, but there never was any confirmation of this.

There was no trouble getting a job in one of the larger commercial shops.

Application to join Sam Barraclough's City Band as trombonist was approved and this resulted in a rewarding experience. Its membership was limited to 36 players, nearly all of whom were professional musicians from the orchestras of the city's legitimate, comedy and vaudeville theatres. It is not at all strange that some of the players were doing a bit of moonlighting as well. There were three other printers in the band.

One felt humble in the midst of these well-trained men, some of whom were Conservatory of Music graduates, who could run through overture numbers such as "Poet and Peasant," "Morning, Noon and Night in Vienna," "William Tell" and other standard classics with all the ease, accuracy and confidence that their skill and talent provided. Or turn to a Sousa march and render it with all the power and sparkle it demanded; or barely breathe into their instruments for whispering accompaniments to vocal soloists.

It was embarrassing at first to be handed the score of a march selection that was completely new, just prior to going on a parade. But it was a challenge and the knack of sight reading had to be acquired, at least to the degree required by the average grade of music performed.

The musical calibre of the band secured for it a month's engagement at the World's Fair at Buffalo, New York.

Later, Mr. Barclay, my Souris employer, was unable to secure all the help he required and I was urged to return.

Really, it did not require much persuasion. There was little warmth in city life. Best friends and acquaintances might live miles distant, making visits something to be planned ahead. There were no spontaneous drop-ins such as one would take for granted in a small town. Distances were time-consuming handicaps. There was loneliness in seeing few other than strange faces. The ever-present friendliness and familiarity of the country had been sorely missed.

So back to Souris I went. A year later, when *The Elgin Banner* was offered for sale I purchased the business, including the printing plant and the house in which it was located. The total price paid was but a meagre fraction of the amount that would be required today as a down payment on a house. But at that time it seemed a lot of money.

I was then 19 years of age.

RE RATIONING DURING THE WAR

It may help you to stop worrying about rationing if you just keep in mind that our forefathers existed without:

Sugar until the 13th century.
Coal fires until the 14th.
Buttered bread until the 15th.
Potatoes and tobacco until the 17th.
Puddings until the 18th.
Gas, matches and electricity until the 19th.
Cars and canned goods until the 20th.

The old boys managed to get along fairly well.

—W. J. REDMOND in *The Maple Creek News*, 1943.

Chapter 8

FIRST NEWSPAPER

A thrill always comes with the acquiring of a new possession to the degree of desire preceding it. It would seem that there is still a deeper enthusiasm accompanying the purchase of a business of a type to which one is deeply committed.

The responsibilities which come with business ownership fade in the presence of a newly created zeal (or could it all be caused by inexperience?) and the challenge of converting dreams into reality.

In retrospect the acquisition of *The Elgin Banner* was a very minor deal, yet at the time was on a par with many other weekly newspapers in respect to plant, property and dollar volume of turn-over.

Elgin was then a village of about 250 people. In the trading area, the farm population was about six persons to the square mile. There were three other newspapers within 12 miles and four others within 20 to 25 miles. Not long afterwards four of these went out of business.

In spite of small populations, the villages involved were quite prosperous because every dollar the farmer parted with (other than those collected by banks and loan companies) was initially spent in these little centres. It was the advent of the automobile and improved roads that shrivelled them all.

People were just learning of the name of the T. Eaton Company and its mail order method of doing business. It was all so new and strange with Toronto a long distance away.

The plant of *The Elgin Banner* included the old hand-operated press that had formerly served *The Souris Plaindealer* at which office it had been tendered a sincere farewell

48

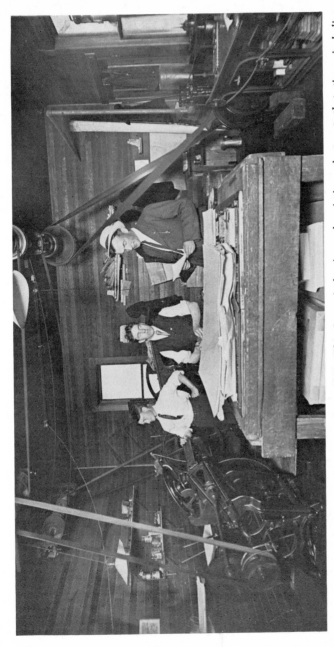

Interior of Maple Creek News office about 1912. This is typical of rural printing plants at that time, including small stationary gasoline engine with exhaust pipe running through back wall, Gordon press, newspaper press (almost hidden in background), overhead shafts, cone pulleys and belting. W. J. Redmond is the man wearing a straw hat.

JAMES GREENBLAT
Swift Current

W. J. REDMOND
Maple Creek

Distinctive front of Weyburn Review office.

2

DAILY

Courier.

VOL. I.　　　MOOSOMIN, MARCH 7, 1885.　　　No. 1.

THE LATEST DESPATCHES CAUGHT FLYING!

N.W.T. WAR!

REIL'S REBELS !

The Duck Lake Fight.

A Fort Qu'Appelle despatch says:—Eleazea Montgrand, a friendly half-breed, who has worked on the old trail to Prince Albert for many years as a teamster has arrived at Fort Qu'Appelle from Clark's Crossing. He confirms the previous report that the Indians north of the South Saskatchewan are uneasy. Bearby, One Arrow, Okemasis and other leading men smoked with Riel's agents before the fight on Beardy's reserve at Duck Lake. Montgrand gives this as an authentic account of tnat engagement.

Major Crozier intended to secure the supplies in Stobart, Eden & Co's. store at Duck Lake, to-gether with a quantity of Government stores that were lying there, destined for Mr. Chaffee, who has charge of the Indian farm near Duck Lake. The rebels, 220 strong under F. Dumont, brother of Dumont the ferryment at Dumont's crossing had, however, raided these stores before Crozier's arrival. Crozier came upon Dumont's force on Beardy's reserve, and called to them to surrender. His men getting the word of command, pointed their rifles at the rebles, who are standing on the edge of a small coulee rub poplar.

Dumont shouted—"Is it to be a fight ?" Crozier answered—"I must shoot if you do not lay down your arms.

Without further parley the rebels dropped into the coulee and leveled their rifles along the top. A whiteman was among them. Crozier, who was 300 yards away held up his hand and the police and volunteers extended their ranks. Both parties fired almost to-gether. The first volley from the half-breeds appeared to be directed at Crozier's left, where the Prince Albert volunteers were stationed, and eight of them fell. The police replied with great vigor, but the men then shouted to Crozier that they could not see the rebels. After the second volly from the rebels Crozier's force began to withdraw, carrying with them the dead and wounded. It was snowing. The police are said to have had two cannon, but Montgrand's informant who saw the fight, says he did not see them

---

A rare historic item. Front page of the first issue of The Moosomin Daily "Courier".

CAMERON R. MCINTOSH
North Battleford

DAVE BELBECK
Swift Current

THE FOUR FAMOUS SAMS
S. R. Moore, Swift Current; S. N. Wynn, Yorkton;
S. J. Dornan, Alameda; S. J. Latta, Govan.

4

BERT McKay
Moosomin

R. S. REID
Kindersley

ROBERT A. TELFER, *founder of The Humboldt Journal*

S. M. Bonneau
Gravelbourg

Phil Flude
Indian Head

W. Morphy
Biggar

Frank Letkemann
Rosthern

J. A. Ives
Tisdale

Joe Ives
Tisdale

Hudson Bay "Post-Review" office in the Moose Capital of the World.

6

Honorary degree of LL.D. being conferred by University of Saskatchewan on S. N. Wynn, of Yorkton. Former Governor-General of Canada, The Hon. Vincent Massey, seen in background, was similarly honored.

S. C. LANCASTER
Melfort

R. S. SQUIRES
Wadena

KEN MAYHEW
Yorkton

7

S. J. DORNAN
1923-1947

WALTER ASHFIELD
1947-1953

SECRETARY-
MANAGERS

MRS. JESSIE DALES
1959-1967

SASKATCHEWAN
WEEKLY
NEWSPAPERS
ASSOCIATION

JOHN A. VOPNI
1953-1959

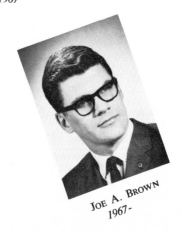

JOE A. BROWN
1967-

8

at the time it was replaced by the cylinder press. The farewell included hopes and wishes that it or another of its kind would never be seen again. But it served the purpose of turning out the small weekly circulation of *The Banner*. One made do with things at hand.

The plant was located in a house which architecturally was a copy of hundreds of other houses built at that time just as present day residences are only slightly different shaped peas in the same pod. The plant and business office took up the ground floor. There were three bedrooms upstairs. It had no basement, was heated by coal stoves with coal oil lamps for illumination.

The title *"Banner"* seemed an ill-fitting name for a weekly newspaper but there were others in the same off-beam category throughout Manitoba, including *Blade, Hustler, Pioneer, Mountaineer, Signal* and *Maple Leaf*. Still, the majority ran standard titles with "*Herald*" leading, "*News*" next following, and then in order "*Times*" and "*Gazette*" and others, appropriate labels for newspapers.

Those were somewhat difficult times for the papers in small places, even though it did not require very much dollar turnover to pay the operating costs. Wages were low and living costs in comparison. There were no taxes other than on real property in the local field.

On the other hand, advertising rates were low—probably as high as the businessmen could afford to pay—and there was little variation in volume of advertising from week to week. Retail business was a sedate sort of thing.

Advertising splurges with cut price bargains were only being tried out by city stores. Foodstuffs were mainly stocked in bulk. An order for such as five cents worth of pepper caused no embarrassment to customer or store management. The clerk would scoop the pepper out of a large tin container and weigh the exact amount in a paper sack, fold down its top and tie the little package with a piece of light cord.

Cans filled with oil for lamps would be made leak-proof by pressing a potato on the spout. Shelves were filled with yard goods of cotton and wool to be made into dresses and other garments for the females of the families. Into their homes dressmakers moved to room and board while the work was being done. Crackers came in barrels—not cardboard boxes.

Job printing was the most profitable part of the country newspaper business but businessmen had only the simplest of stationery requirements. Municipal accounts were among the best. That was before specialization by city firms took most of it away.

The use of loose leaf ledger and account sheets, replacing the old solidly bound book, was still in its infancy.

Provincial and federal voter's lists were profitable to print but such jobs were often spaced years apart.

The first printing job *The Banner's* new management received is well remembered. It was an auction sale bill for W. J. Maguire, an auctioneer, who gave the new owner quite a lift in more ways than one by paying for it in cash on delivery.

Most auctioneers had eccentricities which gave them publicity. Maguire's was that of being a chain cigar smoker, making him the subject of widespread comment; such was most unusual at a time when pipes were more commonly used, and very few hand or factory made cigarettes were smoked.

To most people there was a lot of glamour about a country printing office and its newspaper. It was a business of which they were ignorant in every respect. The converting of written copy into printed sheets was a puzzling process unless they witnessed it from start to finish. All of this put the business on a special pedestal in a community. The responsibility of retaining the respect so accorded rested entirely with the newspaper owner.

It was not in the least unusual for the editor to become the confidant of others and it was also heartening for the young newspaperman to receive suggestions tendered in the most kindly way by those whose experience had clarified their thinking and given rise to sound judgement on matters of some importance.

It is in small towns that folk with marked differences from average or normal, in habits, manner of speech or emotions, acquire prominence. These people are usually referred to as "characters," which designation unfortunately carries an inference that they are queer or peculiar. Actually they are, under the skin, good people. They simply act and do things differently from the common manner.

One of Elgin's characters was a justice of the peace. The conduct of his hearings was carried out in a rather casual manner with an absence of formality or dignity other than that of administering the oath to witnesses. At times these almost became like family discussions as though in search of a finding that might make everyone happy, the guilty ones included. It was this that earned for him the classification in which he was placed.

In contrast to the easy atmosphere and every-day language of the hearing, his decisions were unusually direct and clear cut, given in language more in keeping with that of a brilliant judge than that which he used at all other times.

It was the editor who was facetiously informed of his secret store of wisdom. A case that had any aspects which were in the least bit unusual, he would, before the date of hearing, do some private investigation of his own. This was a simple matter where everyone knew nearly everyone else. Through casual conversation with all persons involved in any way, or were aware of any circumstance connected with the case, he obtained all the evidence that would be given at the hearing anyway.

This he would condense into its salient points, phone the attorney-general's department in Winnipeg, tell them the story and have their decision sent out to him the next day by mail. Thus the verdict in such cases was already decided upon before the case was ever heard, yet completely in accord with all the evidence finally presented at the hearing. It was a sure fire procedure. In none of the few cases appealed were his decisions ever reversed.

All the years in Elgin were happy ones. No more suitable place could have been found in which to receive training in the operation of a newspaper. True, there was nothing specially eventful in the field of news, but there was enough variety to give good scope in news writing experience. There was opportunity to get basic training in the keeping of records and the soliciting of business and the virtue in keeping dead-lines and appointments. And not the least important the financing. Altogether it provided opportunity to acquire a broadening knowledge of business management, writing and printing techniques.

Experience became the sole teacher. The pupil gained in knowledge and understanding through the study and appli-cation of the lessons taught.

In a sense, all business of those days was based on nickels and dimes. Dollars were simply a multiplication of these and the old saying of a penny saved was a penny earned was never more true.

For most people the need for thrift was always present. Such was a good thing. It kept the price of commodities close to their real worth.

It also called for doing without many of the things which in modern times are termed absolutely necessary even to a low standard of living. Today thrift may be practiced by the purchase of a black and white TV instead of a color one. A comparison in those early days could be found in the pur-chase of a wrought iron, small utilitarian heating stove instead of a large massive one loaded with beautiful shiny nickel-plated ornamentation.

A striking example, though a bit unusual, of what thrift could do came up during my stay in Elgin, when a partly trained printer with a wife and two children practically forced his services on me. He was one of an evangelistic sect which had quite a following in and around the village and so had determined to live there. The families clothing needs were simple and the sect practiced "tithing."

At the time all I needed was an apprentice, but when he finally pressured me into admitting that I could afford to pay seven dollars a week, without hesitation he took the job. I raised him to eight dollars. A year later, following the death of his father, he received $200 from the estate. With this he made a down payment on the purchase of a house. A few years later he owned the plant and business of *The Elgin Banner*!

Though everyone worked long hours, each was happy

and contented with time still remaining for recreation. Elgin had a lacrosse team and baseball team. The latter was just beginning to move in and replace the former. Maybe the decline in participation in lacrosse was the imperative need of physical development sufficient to play it with any worthwhile degree of skill and endurance. The players had to be fast runners with plenty of stamina for sixty minutes of play.

There were tennis courts at which a few women, still attired in long skirts, played mixed doubles, making such occasions more of a social nature rather than exhibitions of brisk physical exertion.

In winter, skating, hockey and curling took over. There were house parties with parlor games.

The village had a small brass band, one of the few in a large area. It filled many holiday engagements requiring time-consuming drives in horse-drawn democrats, the most wearying part being the return trip in the darkness of night over miles of rough prairie trails.

There was a small orchestra capable of providing music for the two or three big dances of the year.

There were four churches, some with mid-week prayer meetings. Each had a choir practice every week, faithfully attended by all members.

Any newcomer to the village who attended church was quickly assessed on two points—could he or she sing, follow a tune or sing a part with some degree of accuracy. On passing this unannounced test an invitation to join that particular church's choir would be immediately extended.

At the first practice I attended of the choir of the church I belonged to, I was attracted by a slender, vivacious young woman, with sparkling eyes and a face that revealed a keen personality. She was a teacher on the local school staff.

Three years later Mabel Stirling and I were married to begin fifty-seven years of happiness together—years that were enriched by her unselfishness, her understanding, her sense of humor, her good judgement and her loyalty to family tradition—a wonderful woman, wife and mother.

Chapter 9

MOVE TO SASKATCHEWAN

A year later, an opportunity came to sell *The Elgin Banner* to Gordon A. McMorran who at that time was employed by *The Western Canadian*, published at Manitou, Man. Incidentally, a few years later he purchased *The Souris Plaindealer* from W. J. Barclay to begin a career in public service, fraternal work and historical research that brought him outstanding recognition.

Following the sale, I began to look for a new location. The call of the west was in the air, stimulated by the vast immigration which was pouring thousands of families into the new provinces of Saskatchewan and Alberta.

New towns were advertising openings for newspapers. Some owners were wanting to sell their businesses. There was movement and action everywhere—an unrest brought on by the excess of opportunities bringing illusions of bigger and better things somewhere beyond the ken of impatient individuals.

But how was one to assess the future of any town on the far-flung railway lines in unproven countryside? Nearly all of them were of mushroom growth, with business whetted by the incoming rush of new capital and a bountiful harvest of grain from first crops on fertile prairie soil.

How long would this prosperity last? What towns were most likely to develop into larger centers? How could one facing this new experience make the right selection?

One town in southern Alberta looked promising. A liberal advertising guarantee for one year was offered. The adjacent fields carried lush and healthy crops. But a hunch that this was not the place persisted—a hunch that was fortunately observed.

That crop was the only one the arid district had for some years and not too long afterwards a prairie fire swept into the town which was lacking in water supply and fire fighting equipment. Nearly one half of the buildings were destroyed creating a loss from which it never recovered.

Another place visited was where the newspaper was for sale. The owner kept no books or records so he had no way of accounting the value of his plant or business.

There was an opportunity to buy a half interest in a two-partner ownership of a small daily newspaper in one of the smaller cities. Negotiations fell through because the other partner overvalued his talents too highly and would not agree to a fifty-fifty split on profits.

These examples were characteristic of the ferment that was going on under the guise of progress and prosperity.

Finally, after much travelling and personal enquiry, what appeared to be the best location was finally selected. It was in Rouleau, Saskatchewan where *The Rouleau Enterprise* was owned by a company of local businessmen. This group had purchased it from one of two partners who had made some sort of deal with his compatriot just previous to the latter's sudden departure from the town. This event was highlighted by the fact that the wife of the hotel clerk had gone with him, leaving no address. No one seemed too anxious to talk about it.

The company did not want to carry on a business about which all the shareholders knew nothing. These men had simply stepped into the situation to let it be understood that such goings-on were not to be tolerated in their town.

The *Enterprise* plant was a tidy little one located in the basement of a brick block, a location that had one drawback. Every time there was a rain the water would run down the entrance steps into the basement and flood the floor, at times to a depth of two inches.

Rouleau, like other Soo Line towns, was throbbing that summer, not only with the influx of settlers mainly from Kansas, Nebraska and Iowa, but from Ontario. A more capable group of experienced farmers would have been hard to find anywhere.

Every freight train dropped off immigrant cars carrying horses, implements and household goods. These were quickly unloaded by the owners and moved out to the land previously bought from land companies at prices considerably less per acre than they had sold their original holdings for. They were richer through capital gain. Everyone carried a cheque book in his hip pocket.

Until freeze-up, horses and plows kept turning over the virgin sod to make fields ready for seeding the next spring.

A few steam tractors of 70 to 100 horsepower with eight and nine foot diameter drive wheels were at work mainly on custom jobs. They pulled ten and twelve furrow gang plows and could break a quarter section of land in a few hours. When viewed from a distance the puffs of black smoke billowing silently from the stacks of these coal fired giants, on a quiet, calm, sunlit summer day, created a picturesque scene against a background of far-away horizon, blue sky and white clouds.

The small 10 to 20 horsepower gasoline tractors were just coming into use. Farmers found the heavy gumbo soil of the Regina plains a severe test for them.

Yet here for all to see was the infancy of a revolution in farm methods and practice. The work horse was soon to be pushed out of the picture. Power machinery, large in work capacity, drawn by gasoline and diesel tractors with ever-increasing power on their drawbars were rapidly taking over.

It was the time when the internal combustion engine had graduated from its first function as a stationary power plant and entered the mobile field. In a few years this progressive step had almost completely changed the old work methods of farming. It also brought into being, via the automobile, an era of mass travel and transport.

It was indeed a priceless experience for those living in those days to witness the birth and the early years of the mechanical age, followed by its progression into a period of amazing invention and scientific discovery of hitherto mysterious sources of power.

Three express trains each day, back and forth, were evidence of the commercial boom in progress. There were people with plenty of money for investment in business as well as in agriculture.

Rouleau was not the only little hamlet on the Soo Line from North Portal to Moose Jaw that in a year or so suddenly expanded with almost frantic growth. American capital sprinkled offices of new banks, grain and lumber companies along its mileage. Shrewd investors felt they could forecast the wealth that the rich soil of the Regina plains would produce.

The town of Rouleau was setting the pace in public ownership of utilities. Good water was almost impossible to get anywhere in the gumbo land area. In most localities, drinking water was drawn in wagon tanks, from wells or creeks varying distances away, and sold by the barrel.

Eavestroughing that poured rain water into stout barrels supplied the need for other household purposes during the summertime, while snow and ice took care of winter requirements. All of it was the softest water one could desire.

The town had drilled two wells and found an ample supply of water at 200 feet depth. An electric light plant, a pumping station and water mains were installed in a suitable building to make Rouleau one of the most modern towns for many miles around.

Business establishments supplying every need crowded both sides of a block on Main Street and spilled around the corners onto other streets. There were real estate men and horse traders. There were livery barns which rented out horses and rigs to drive land seekers into the country.

There was a hotel with rooms that were filled each night and sometimes with cots in its hallways. There were two doctors, a lawyer, an undertaker, pool rooms, a race track, race horses and even the odd poker game to which a newcomer might be invited by the group of regular participants.

There were four churches and an excellent public school, for the majority of the citizens had strong religious belief and firm conviction that church worship and good basic education were essentials in building a better individual and community life.

The combination of assets contained in Rouleau business and social life made it a most desirable place in which to live.

Though housing was at a premium, the scales were tipped slightly in favor of the new newspaperman and so we were able to buy a house that had just been completed. It was a two and a half storey structure of architectural lines greatly admired at the time, but which would be shunned today.

Like most others, it was located on a bare lot on a street which ended on a prairie trail winding its way along a road allowance, half hidden in a thick growth of prairie grass and continuing beyond the horizon.

It was in this house that Mabel and I lived for thirty-four years during which time our five children were born to add to our happiness, which was further enhanced by the gracious atmosphere of friendliness and neighborliness so consistent with the spirit of the pioneers.

Chapter 10

CHANGING SCENE

One year after the purchase of *The Rouleau Enterprise*, the expanding business activity of the town through increased urban and rural population put a strain on the mechanical resources of the printing plant. More floor space was needed to accommodate more equipment. The local Masonic Lodge also needed more commodious and convenient quarters so it built a two-storey temple building. The second storey became its lodge room while *The Enterprise* leased the ground floor for its new home.

A second-hand Cottrell drum cylinder press was installed, also a folding machine and a larger gasoline stationary engine. A little later, it became quite evident that the hand-setting of type for news and advertising was no longer economical, so a well-used typesetting machine was purchased.

Incidentally, this old machine sparked a story of the type oft repeated by those belonging to specific occupational groups.

The name given to the machine by its manufacturers was "monoline." This to a degree described the nature of its product which was one solid bar of lead, or one line of type. On the top of this bar was cast letters to form the words assembled by the operator as he "set up" the weekly news. It was the "slugs" so cast that filled the news columns of the newspaper pages.

The monoline was an attempt to provide a typesetting machine at low cost and at one time many of them were used throughout Canada. Unfortunately it had many mechanical weaknesses. It had to be given careful attention with special care in the adjustment of many parts. Lacking this, it could cause much trouble in operation.

One morning it had been giving our operator plenty of worry and annoyance just at the time when he was trying to meet our deadline. He was a nervous, highly strung young man, and he was frustrated almost beyond endurance.

While he sat operating the keyboard, an outsider came in, and with keen interest watched the operator's finger-work for a while. He then quite pleasantly remarked: "It just works like a typewriter, doesn't it?"

The operator's control of his feelings snapped right then. Jumping up from his chair, he grabbed it and swung it up over his shoulder shouting: "Work's like a typewriter? Hell!" Then bringing the chair down with all his strength, he smashed it into complete wreckage.

The stranger was nowhere to be seen a few seconds after that occurred.

There was nothing unusual about the growth of The Enterprise at that time. The same progress was being duplicated many times over by weekly newspapers in most small and growing towns on the prairies. Business came to these offices without solicitation. The number of pages of most weekly issues were increased, and maybe page sizes were increased also.

Subscription lists grew in size as new farmers arrived. The Enterprise began to print weekly newspapers for three other towns without any special canvassing or solicitation.

The pressure of reporting, editing and management, plus a shift in the plant to assist in getting forms ready to meet deadlines made it evident that the owner of a small business could not do all the work and supervision required of him in an eight-hour day or a five-day week—a fact that many businessmen of today will agree is still as true as it ever was.

Certainly, a day's duties did not end at six o'clock. Evening meetings and other events had to be attended if they were to be reported on fully and accurately. Many were the evenings that the head of the family was absent from home.

Quite naturally, all of this was not monotonous. There

were peaks of special news interest to spark flagging activity, yet strangely enough that which was really a highlight slipped into the passing picture without being fully recognized at the time.

The first poems written by Edna Jaques were published in *The Rouleau Enterprise.*

Miss Jaques was in her mid-teens when the urge to picture in poetic form the simplicity of rural life with all its homely virtues, started her on the path which brought her recognition as one of Canada's most expressive poets.

She lived fourteen miles from Rouleau near the village of Briercrest and it was a natural decision on her part to send her first compositions to the nearest local newspaper.

Shortly after, when daily newspapers and farm journals began to accept her writings, a market developed for them providing her with some monetary compensation. Then, as her poems were printed farther afield, her talent became fully recognized. It is probably not generally known that quotations from some of Edna Jaques' poems are to be found on American Legion Buildings in the United States.

The large number of weekly newspaper offices that had opened put a premium on help. While the average competent employee would stay permanently on a staff, sometimes extra printers were needed, and those available often turned out to be of the "tramp" printer variety. Even though the thrill of wandering from town to town had then almost disappeared, a few of the itinerant ones remained. They were often called "boomers."

Most of these roving tradesmen were quite proficient, but usually they had a major weakness—a thirst for alcoholic beverages. One morning an employee who had been on the staff for over a month failed to turn up for work. It was late in the afternoon when he made an appearance, an appearance that few missed. Down the main street he weaved, singing at the top of his voice "With Rings on My Fingers and Bells on My Toes," his own parody of a popular song of the day.

It was not a good advertisement for *The Enterprise.*

Businessmen generally were quite prompt in paying their

monthly accounts, though some merchants pressured the printer to carry contra accounts with them. This was a pattern closely related to blackmail, and, unfortunately, all too many weekly newspaper publishers fell for this unsound practice in order to secure as much business as they could for themselves.

Possibly some of the merchants had financing problems and were short of ready cash, for it was common practice for farm customers of all retail establishments to run charge accounts for as long as ten months with payment being made in the fall after they had threshed their crop and marketed some of it. Those were the days when grain was generally sold for spot cash . . . no initial, interim and final payment system.

There was no orderly marketing of grain at that time. There was no such thing as quotas, such as came later under the control of the Canadian Wheat Board—a system which brought many benefits to all grain growers.

Immediately after threshing, every farmer rushed his grain to the local elevators, or took the alternative of loading cars directly from wagons or trucks to save the cost of handling charges by the elevator companies.

Later the grain would be sold on the Winnipeg Grain Exchange, through a member company.

This rush in grain marketing was brought about by the credit system then in vogue. The farmer was anxious to pay the stores, implement and oil dealers, notes at the bank and other financial obligations he had incurred after the proceeds of the previous harvest had all been spent.

The situation was such that during the months of October, November and December, cash money was plentiful and changed hands rapidly as farmers first, and then businessmen in turn discharged their liabilities.

Because of this credit system which a one-crop economy established, these months contained the main pay days of the entire year. During the summer months, very little cash changed hands, other than that passed on by the few working for wages or on salary.

One group that was quite undeservedly embarrassed

by this were the clergy. Usually they had to stretch their personal credit during the cashless days of summer with the local merchants, until the flood of money began to flow in the fall, when individual donations to churches would be paid in one lump sum.

Weekly contribution envelopes were never thought of. In fact, it took years to bring them into general use.

This entire situation provided a background for a local incident reflecting several timely facets, including the free and easy western valuation placed on dollars as compared with the thrifty, careful attitude of eastern Canadian people.

It was in August that the pastor of one of Rouleau's churches found himself in urgent need of some cash. He had not received any of his stipend for some months.

He voiced his plea and a meeting of the board of managers was called. It was held in the front store part of a harness shop owned by one of the board members who shall be known as Dan.

Two or three chairs and wooden boxes of various sizes providing the seating, and in the crowded space some leaned back amid harness hanging on the wall or found horse collars comfortable rests for their heads.

There was the usual preliminary chatting and laughing over matters of common everyday interest in a bourgeois manner of speech somewhat out of tune with what might be expected at such a meeting. Some who had just come from their fields were in work clothes, unshaven and dust covered.

Actually their rough appearance and speech completely belied their true character. At heart they were all good, sincere and upright folk.

A general discussion of the church's financial condition led to the main purpose of the meeting. The chairman spoke out with "well, we had better start a subscription list. Gimme a sheet of paper and a pencil."

Dan finally came up with these. The chairman scribbled his name with some figures after it and passed it on to the one next to him. It continued to be passed from one to another, each person signing his name followed by figures. The paper finally reached the hands of Dan's 'teenage brother who had just arrived from Ontario that morning. He too followed the pattern by adding his name and figures.

At this point Dan quickly said: "Here, let me see that paper." On scanning it he added, "Mac, I think you have gone a bit strong on this."

Mac replied that he had always supported his church in the east, and as he was going to make his home in Rouleau he felt it was only his duty to the church there.

Dan pointed out that he still thought Mac had promised too much for a young fellow who had not even got a job, to which Mac replied, quite calmly: "Well, if the others can give one dollar or seventy-five cents, I guess I should be good for twenty-five cents."

"Hell" snorted Dan, "them figures is dollars, not cents and just to teach you a lesson not to work too fast in a new country, I'm going to see that you pay it." And he did.

The free and easy western attitude towards money was first engendered by the movement of large amounts of cash brought in by American farmers and investors together with lavish returns from grain crops during the first few years that the countryside opened up.

Areas in the west with a big development in power farming had still to become acquainted with the frugality characteristic of the east.

The idea of one-cent coins ever being used was scoffed by the westerners. Nickels were the smallest coin they used. Pennies were never seen. Charges, such as freight bills, carrying odd cents were all settled on the five-cent basis. A two-cent overage was never paid while a three-cent one was taken care of with a nickel. This play resulted in total charges being within a few cents of total collected.

It was only when department stores in cities began to sell goods at odd cent prices, such as ninety-nine cents, that coppers came into general use.

Advertising rates in weekly newspapers at this time were in accord with the general practice of having nothing to do with pennies. If ever the rates were increased, five cents or a multiple of that sum would be added to the previous rate.

This was before the adoption of the "agate line" measure-ment of 14 lines to the column inch in depth which called for a charge per line and doing away with a charge per inch.

When this became standard practice with advertising agencies placing newspaper advertising, country weeklies had to comply. Most of the western weeklies made the change around 1920. However, most weekly newspapers still quote the local rate on the inch basis even though such is based on a rate per line. This brings out such rates as fifty-six cents per inch or eighty-four cents per inch. The pennies eventually won out.

When the advantages of using the line rate began to be impressed on newspaper publishers at the annual conventions, the subject provided considerable scope for argument on the part of Charlie Hinds, of Lumsden, Sask. Charlie was a genial soul with bushy white hair and heavy moustache which made him look a lot like Mark Twain, though he would have laughed derisively had such an idea ever been suggested to him.

He could be counted on to liven things up when a dull spell showed signs of forming during a discussion period. At times he appeared to be good-naturedly stubborn, but those who got to know him intimately realized that if his quips and quirks did not provide amusement for others he was having a quiet chuckle to himself. He would not hesitate to produce ideas contrary to his own opinions just to get discussions moving.

At a convention, Charlie would just wait for someone to say that the new way to charge for advertising space was by the line and that there were 14 lines to the inch.

With some heat he would at once declare there never was a size of type manufactured of which 14 lines would make 72 points or one inch. Five point type made 70 points and $5\frac{1}{2}$-point type made 77 points to the inch.

So far as he was concerned it was all just a smart trick to try to make advertisers feel they were getting more for their money, because 1400 lines sounded more than 100 inches. He declared he had always been told that there were 12 lines to the inch of 6 point type and that was that.

Back home in his office, however, when cheques would come in from agencies in payment of national advertising accounts he would smile a little and say: "Well, those smart young fellows down east have paid me for two extra lines in every inch."

Actually it caused the weekly newspaperman no trouble to adopt the agate line charge and following the first world war it fitted in with a strong upsurge in national advertising in their papers. The largest buyers of advertising space then were automobile manufacturers, including some whose names have long since disappeared from the public eye.

Pictures and descriptions of early models of these cars to be found in weekly newspaper files provide a permanent anthology that is both exciting and enlightening.

Allow me here to say that the pernicious dime novel always pictures the Indian scout as a cold blooded fiend, revelling in deeds of gore. In respect of our scouts this is a great mistake—a gross calumny. They are the quietest, most unostentatious and tender-hearted men in the country.

—P. G. LAURIE, *Saskatchewan Herald*,
Battleford, Sask.

Chapter 11

GOOD LUCK

Owners of country printing offices produced weekly newspapers and also some commercial printing. From the very beginning, whether they recognized it or not, they were in all likelihood to be faced with a dwindling volume of business.

The only exceptions to this have been in the larger towns with more central locations. As these latter towns grew larger through drawing business from a wider area, the smaller towns became still smaller.

The automobile and good roads played an important part in hastening this centralization of business.

Thus every printing plant and newspaper owner in these smaller towns, who observed this business trend, could only realize that his future was becoming less and less secure.

He was also being faced with a growing competition in job printing items in every day use by city firms producing specialized work. Loyalty of home town customers could only be stretched to a certain dollar point.

The small town printer was not in a position to enter into a specialized business of his own for the range of products was already well covered by well established companies with enormous investments in buildings, plants and a corps of trained salesmen—something which he could not duplicate.

In this connection it was only through a chance encounter I became aware of the immense possibilities in a specialized line of printing which otherwise I would never have dreamed of producing. In fact it was a type of work that the owner of any small country newspaper plant would have shied away from. But it became the backbone of my commercial printing department.

The accepted definition of the word "chance", or its synonyms "luck" and "good fortune," usually reads: "something that befalls as a result of unknown and unconsidered forces."

Human beings know that the rising and setting of the sun, the moon and the stars operate on a rigid schedule.

With continuing intensified research into the presence of living things on the earth, scientists have proven the reality of fundamental natural laws controlling life in all its phases.

There are basic laws which if ignored by individuals or nations, inevitably inflict their own punishment.

There are laws which determine the nature and creation and use of electrical, atomic and other forms of power.

During every minute of our days we are surrounded and patrolled by laws which determine our way of life.

Yet with the keenest minds constantly searching for a fuller knowledge and understanding of the rules which control the pattern, no one has been able to diagnose what determines how, why and when luck—good or bad—comes swooping down on an individual without warning of any kind.

Maybe this is the one weak link in the chain of rigid rules which frame the great universal plan of all creation. Or is it the exception that proves the rule?

Theologians of Calvanistic belief have an explanation for the unexpected arrival of good, or bad luck, or fortune. It is known as predestination.

As always, this topic could initiate a lengthy discussion which once more would most likely fail to uncover the basic rule applicable in all cases, other than good luck could be a reward and bad luck a punishment.

In many cases, what is casually called good, or bad fortune has a reason. Somewhere, sometime, the person involved may have taken some action to produce the long-range result—an action which may have faded from memory. Actually, such an example could not be classified as luck.

Yet no other word than "luck" would describe what

happened to me at Rouleau, Saskatchewan in the year 1912. Certainly I had nothing to do with creating the circumstance which produced the rare development that followed.

An advance agent of a theatrical company arrived in town to book the public hall and post advertising matter announcing its appearance.

His coming, along with his immediate troubles, created the beginning of a unique business with a continent-wide scope and reputation. That business became more than a lusty partner to the little weekly newspaper I was then publishing.

I had never seen the man before, or even heard of his company which was an excellent one out of Chicago.

Why did such a fine company decide to fill an open date at Rouleau, on its way to Regina to begin a tour of the C. P. Walker chain of theatres in the three prairie provinces?

Why did the American printer fail to ship the required posters in good time?

Why did the railway company fall down on its usually prompt transportation service?

Such matters were completely out of my control. It was all just plain good fortune, coming without apparent reason.

The agent's posters were three days late in arriving. During that time, he was in and out of my office several times a day, trying to cool off his impatience and no doubt appreciating the little bit of show talk I could carry on.

He wondered why there was not a poster printing plant somewhere in that part of Canada from which a prompt and convenient service could be obtained.

Jestingly, I said: "What about starting one here?"

He thought for a moment and said, "why not."

I suddenly had a lot of ideas in opposition to my own suggestion, the main one being that Rouleau was but a small town sitting out on the wide-open prairie. He retaliated with reasons sound enough to nullify my objections and finished up by pointing out that so long as a poster plant was located at a place which had a good train service, that was the main consideration. Anyway, most showmen never visited the plants which produced their posters.

At that time two express trains each day, back and forth, passed through Rouleau providing close connections, west, north and east with main line Canadian Pacific Railway trains.

We met that evening for a more detailed assessment of the idea. His knowledge of the overall poster printing situation and his conclusions convinced me that a paying volume of business could be built up in serving travelling road shows. No consideration was given at the time to supplying the needs of other types of entertainment.

I was almost completely ignorant of the styles and quantities of paper used by show companies. I did not even know the size of a "show" one-sheet, which incidentally is 28 by 42 inches.

So our meeting turned into a school of instruction that lasted until the early morning hours, beginning with a listing of the different sizes of posters, date lines and cards, all specified in the lingo of the show business from snipes and daubs to 28-sheet billboards.

It was interesting to learn that all these sizes had been standardized for years—ever since the days when the small train circus had begun to displace the little horse-drawn wagons which slowly meandered from village to village bringing a bit of excitement to rural dwellers.

It was then the astute circus operator began to calculate shrewdly, not only how to capture more dollars, but also how to operate and promote his show more economically.

Part of this efficiency drive was the standardization of poster sizes, in effect the early beginnings of mass production techniques.

Posters and date lines in all the smaller sizes are cut without waste of paper from one-sheets. They are of such dimension that six of one size, three of another and two of another cut evenly out of a one-sheet.

When one remembers that there were just six show days a week, and that date lines were most often (almost exclusively) ordered for a week at a time, such orders could be printed entirely on full sized sheets, with the various sized posters cut apart after the printing was done. This enabled presses to run at full-cylinder size-capacity all the time.

Once this mathematical angle of show printing had been explained to me it was a fairly simple matter to begin selecting sizes and styles of wood type.

All letters one inch in vertical height to several feet high are made of wood, mainly because of lightness in weight.

The smaller sizes are carved on end grain maple, medium and fairly large sizes on side grain maple and the extremely large on basswood.

My first order was naturally not a very large one, but of necessity did include some large figures to be used on date lines.

Showmen had always known the impact of a large figure heralding the date the show would come to town, especially when heavy bill posting met the eye at every turn.

The largest I acquired then covered half the surface of a one-sheet. These were pygmies compared with those bought, or carved ourselves, to make posters with seven-foot square figures which circus bill-posters delighted in plastering on sides of farm barns and empty buildings. It was always said, "they can be seen a mile away."

I had a drum cylinder press which produced my first posters but soon I acquired a two-revolution machine large enough to print a double one-sheet size and this was followed by a pony two-revolution for the smaller posters and half- and one-sheet cards.

At first the only customers we had were those companies which came to put their shows on in Rouleau town hall. Then we were able to make personal contact, show them the plant and its facilities.

These companies were quite numerous, averaging about one a week. As they travelled up and down and across the prairie provinces, using our printing, more and more shows became familiar with our business, as every poster carried our imprint even if it was in small type.

Soon we were printing weekly posters for repertory stock companies playing winter season in theatres in several western cities. This provided a steady volume with equally stable income—a most appreciated phase of any business.

At that time there were five other poster plants scattered

across Canada, at Montreal, Toronto, Chatham (Ontario), Winnipeg and Vancouver. A few years later a firm in Calgary opened a poster department but this did not continue in operation very long.

Our good friend Sam J. Latta, at Govan, Saskatchewan, became intrigued with the business, bought some wood type and picked up a few customers. But since he was situated on a branch railway line with limited and badly-timed connections at its terminal points, he failed to make any headway.

Looking back to those pioneer days when I was striving to expand the market I had discovered by a stroke of luck, I realize now that my inexperience had much to do with my entry into a highly specialized field of printing, already covered by large competitive companies. I had discarded my first belief that a small town was no place to initiate such a business. Now I wonder how many showmen were curious as to the calibre of an outfit that started a city type of business away out in the countryside.

Yet in the end, as it turned out, it was fortunate that I had few misgivings but considerable enthusiasm.

While lack of assurance no doubt at first held back a considerable amount of business, our location had an intense advertising value. People talked about it and the more the business grew the more they talked in wonderment.

Had Enterprise Show Print been set up in Regina, Moose Jaw or Saskatoon, it would have been considered a routine matter without creating much publicity.

I recall an incident in this connection, which happened in later years when our plant was equipped to turn out the "big stuff."

The story involved J. Alex Sloan, of Sloan's Championship Auto Racing, of Chicago. He was instructing his new publicity man, Art Swenson, as to the best methods of promoting his auto thrill show dates in Canada.

He told Art to order all the billboard and other posters from Enterprise Show Print at Rouleau, Saskatchewan and as this would be the first business for him to transact in Canada he would travel direct to that town via the Soo Railway.

72

The last thing Sloan said to Swenson as he saw the latter into his sleeping car in Chicago was: "Now when that train stops there and you get off, don't get back on the train thinking you have gotten off at the wrong town. If the sign on the railway station reads 'Rouleau,' you are at the right place no matter how small it looks to you. The town is a little place with only a one-block business section, sitting out on the flat prairie, but even though its small, that's where they print the biggest date figures in Canada and those are what we want."

My sights at first did not reach farther than Winnipeg on the east and the Rocky Mountains on the west and I was only concerned with theatrical companies.

If anyone had then suggested the time was coming when Enterprise Show Print in the little 800-population town of Rouleau, Saskatchewan would eventually be shipping posters to dramatic companies, musical comedy companies, circuses, carnivals and other users all across Canada from Halifax, (yes, also Newfoundland) to Victoria, B.C., in volume amounting to tons in weight, I would have scoffed at the idea.

Neither would I have taken seriously any prophecy that we would finally be the only poster printing plant operating in Canada, or that we would be making shipments as far south as Kentucky and west to the Pacific coast states.

Yet, all of this did eventually take place.

The conditions which resulted in Enterprise Show Print finally becoming the only poster printing plant in Canada were created mainly by the rapid growth in popularity of moving pictures. With movie theatres springing up in towns as well as cities, the travelling road shows began to disappear. The five other Canadian poster plants were geared only to the production of the smaller-sized posters which were commonly used by such companies, and as the latter thinned out, the printing companies packed their wood type away and concentrated on other kinds of job printing.

It was in 1919 that a second bit of good fortune descended upon us.

This time it could be definitely explained.

A general strike in Winnipeg was gaining strength with

different trades unions joining in.

When the railway expressmen walked off their jobs, the Winnipeg poster plant was unable to accept orders as it could not ship them out.

Shows travelling the prairie provinces who had been getting their work done there immediately began to patronize us. They remained as permanent customers.

By this time I had really become enamoured with the poster business.

There was an unusually fascinating atmosphere about it presenting an excitement and challenge not to be found in the repetitious routine of commercial printing of those days.

Then the showmen, each with a different personality, from the warm-hearted to the extroverts, from the penurious to the free spenders, from the classic to the reformer, from the everyday type of performer to those rich with talent, provided an ever-changing panorama of contacts to keep interest continually aroused.

In the beginning, I suppose I had the somewhat narrow outlook, common to many folk living in small towns and villages. In fact carnivals and circuses with their hundreds of employees seemed huge and overpowering. It seemed they could only be properly served by the large poster plants in the United States, and the kind of business they had, placed them entirely beyond our ability and scope.

However, other new channels had been opened up, through specialization in posters for sports days (every little town in the entire Canadian west used to put on a sports day), dance bands, department stores and fairs and exhibitions.

Beginning in 1914, we sent out catalogues each year to sports day committees and all western fairs and exhibitions.

These illustrated in miniature the various pictorial posters and tack cards we kept in stock ready for immediate imprinting with local copy required. Mail orders became an important factor in our growing volume of business.

At this time, a new department far removed from poster printing was instituted. It was the manufacture of gold stamped rosettes and flat style prize ribbons for fairs. Again we entered a highly competitive field.

A hot stamping press was acquired, together with brass type. The latter is required to produce the sharpest lettering on ribbon, cloth or leather. Ordinary lead type will not long endure the high degree of heat and pressure required to melt the gold leaf and impress the glittering letters into the ribbon fabric.

Several weeks were spent in testing various kinds of gold leaf and ribbon before the operation was standardized so that a top quality product could be turned out on a steady production line basis. Even the seamstresses had to acquire the knack of turning out different styles of rosettes that were perfect circles.

At that time, most of the ribbon orders of western fairs were being placed with eastern Canadian and United States firms. Their loyalty to the new western industry was remarkable. Within two years 75 per cent of the large exhibitions were customers of Enterprise Show Print.

Stores used posters for sales decorations. Exhibitions adopted circus billing methods by sending out billing crews to put up posters and cards on every available spot within their respective drawing areas.

It was only a step from exhibition contacts to that of carnivals which played them. More wood type had to be obtained in still larger sizes along with the big "bull" date figures seven feet square.

With this equipment it was no longer necessary to view circuses with awe. We could supply them with any size of paper or card they demanded and in any quantity they might possibly require, and having some time previously gone into the engraving of wood blocks in intaglio lettering for their date lines, an extra touch adding greatly to the appearance of all their posting paper.

From the time we began to serve circuses there was rarely one that entered Canada, particularly west of the great lakes, that we did not serve. Some were those carrying the old, old names of Hagenbeck-Wallace, Cole Bros., Gentry Bros., Sells-Floto, plus those of more modern times, including Al. G. Barnes, Clyde Beatty, Howe's Great London, all travelling by train.

The fisherman likes to boast of the "big ones" that he hooks but fails to land. We had one such experience which, while it lasted, was an exciting and challenging one.

The general agent of Ringling Bros., Barnum & Bailey Circus, the oldest, largest and most famous of all American circuses, one year offered us the contract for printing their date lines for a full season, stating the price they were willing to pay. It was a rate giving an excellent margin of profit.

At first the offer was not taken seriously by us, though big circus owners are not given to joking in dealing with essentials. After considering all the factors involved, it became apparent the circus boys knew what they were doing.

Canadian money was then at a 10 per cent discount in the United States. The price offered, while below Chicago rates, was still higher than normal Canadian prices. As the circus proposed playing more than half of its season in central and western states, the cost of shipping over the season from our plant would total less than from Chicago.

Before going into the contract, we definitely needed assurance we could obtain extra help and one more cylinder press. A finger was quickly placed on the latter.

When it came to locating manpower, we were beaten, even though only six extra men would have been enough. None were available on the prairies but Vancouver harbored a large number of printers and pressmen who were working only half time. No doubt they had their own good reasons for not accepting our offer of above-union pay rates, railway tickets, subsidized board and room, but not a single one would promise to come.

The contract had to be turned down.

The only edge we had on the fisherman was we knew exactly the weight of the catch that escaped us.

To print paper for New York city and its environs would have taken us two shifts working for twenty days. Chicago paper would have required three days and all other single day dates, one day each. The total value of the contract was almost $90,000.

At the time we swung into carnival printing, Johnny J. Jones was the big wheel in that business on this continent.

Johnny was an undersized Welshman with a small drooping black moustache, looking less like a million-dollar carnie owner than almost anyone else, employee or patron, who might be on his lot at any time.

While always immaculate, he cared little for style or fashion. When occasion required him to go through his midway he appeared somewhat carelessly attired. Usually he was without a coat, making it most evident that he preferred the old-time suspenders to a smart-looking trouser belt. His manner of conversation, though stilted, had a friendly warmth, and at the same time reflected his keen business sense.

He was our first carnival customer, and continued to be until he was bid out of the Western Canada A fair circuit by the rapidly expanding Royal American Shows owned by Carl Sedlmayer.

Physically and sartorially, Carl was just the opposite of Johnny. Of normal height with a somewhat profound bearing and dressed in the latest clothes that good fashion offered, Carl had all the appearance of the successful business-man he was.

So far as we were concerned, Carl simply took over where Johnny left off.

Then among the earlier Canadian carnivals was Conklin & Garrett Shows which first came out of Seattle. We served it until Patty Conklin took over the operation of the Canadian National Exhibition midway at Toronto, when he sold his Conklin Shows to Jimmy Sullivan of Wallace Bros. Shows.

Among other Canadian carnivals who placed their paper orders with us (some of whose names may be unknown to many present-day readers) were Gray's, Sim's, E. J. Casey's, Royal Canadian, Queen City and Bernard & Barry.

Considered elite printing contracts were those for the Coldstream Guards Band and the Royal Air Force Band, of London, England and the Australian National Band. These required multi-colored pictorial posters in keeping with their high musical standards and traditions.

Thrill Shows such as Jimmy Lynch's Death Dodgers, of New York; Aut Swenson's Thrillcade of Springfield, Missouri; Flash Williams Thrill Show of Chicago; Canadian

Death Dodgers of Montreal; Sloan's Championship Auto Racing, of Chicago, and others, were large account customers, so that with the combined business of circuses, carnivals, exhibitions, chautauquas, theatrical companies, sports days and department stores, Enterprise Show Print was firmly established during the early 1920s.

Many personal memories are stirred in recalling the names of so many of these men who were the most successful in their respective fields of entertainment on the North American continent.

With my purchase of *The Estevan Mercury* in 1944, the poster plant was moved from Rouleau to Estevan, from which time the name of Enterprise Show Print was replaced by King Show Print.

Following the close of the Second World War, both the newspaper and the show print business was owned by a partnership of my two sons, Stirling and William, and myself, and employed a staff of 30 to 35 employees.

Chapter 12

MAKING PRINTING HISTORY

An innovation now recorded in the history of printing in Canada, along with other advancements, all combining to picture the scope and progress of the industry, was the first engraving in this country of wood blocks from which multi-colored pictorial posters were printed.

This was done by Enterprise Show Print at Rouleau, and it was the only printing plant in Canada ever to do this type of work.

It is true that some shops did carve a few small cuts on linoleum and some blocks with "intaglio" (white on solid color) lettering, but none attempted the intricate and demanding technique required of the wood engraver in cutting blocks for pictorial posters.

For almost half a century, show printing establishments in the United States, where poster printing was highly specialized, turned out that type of poster.

Before this method was taken up, all pictorial posters were produced by the lithographic process at comparatively high cost for preparatory work.

The use of wood blocks resulted in the reduction of production costs, particularly for pictorial posters.

Wood engraving in the Enterprise Show Print plant was begun in 1914. The skill of hand carving such things as perfectly straight lines and true circles, had to be acquired as well as an intimate knowledge of the entire procedure from original drawings to completed posters ready to be lifted from the delivery table of the printing press.

This knowledge had to be obtained from the study of workmanship detail of other posters and largely through trial and error. There was no one near at hand to teach it and not even one who could advise on the rudimentary requirements and problems connected with the process.

At first we did not even know the proper size of hand chisels required for cutting V- and U-shaped grooves which outlined the picture details, after which the larger blank areas were routed out by a power machine. Then, it had to be learned that a V-tool was more suited for carving a certain style of picture than a U-tool; there were other styles that would call for a U-tool. In a sense, it was only a minor detail to be observed, yet failure to follow this basic technique could be spotted in the completed poster by a keen critic.

Experimentation and experience eventually conquered the technique of hand wood engraving.

We had to learn how best to transfer the drawing to the boards in readiness for carving and separating its colors. Practically all posters were printed in three colors—yellow, red and blue.

A board had to be carved for each color, each carrying only the portions of the picture calling for one of the three specific colors.

A clever artist would be able to draw five-color pictures requiring the use of only three colors of ink. This was accomplished by overprinting, using semi-transparent inks, so that yellow over blue would produce a shade of green, or yellow over red produce orange. This procedure, however, required the printing of the different colors out of normal sequence, so that the artist had to be very careful how he used the colors on his drawing. It also required acquisition of much technical knowledge of printing inks.

All of these details took considerable time to become familiar with in order to get production on a standardized basis.

Getting suitable drawings at first was a real problem. Not every commercial artist had the technique required to draw good poster pictures which called for skill in using masses of color, rather than fine line or intermediate color tints.

Posters are designed for viewing from some distance when

fine lines and delicate color distinctions lose their effect.

Facial expressions and other effects have to be produced by proper shaping and placing of color masses and heavy lines. The skilled poster artist can produce varied expressions of an eye by manipulating three lines and a round spot in various shapings and relative positioning to each other. This type of drawing is simplicity in itself—yet so difficult because of its simplicity.

But in catering to the amusement and entertainment field the choice of available art is further narrowed down. That which is "away out" is taboo.

Correct detail, with a punch and appropriate atmosphere must be definite and unmistakeable. An artist is needed who can picture wild animals, clowns, ferris wheels, horses, acro-bats and other features common to carnivals and circuses, at the peak of their exciting performances.

At first we had to buy our drawings from artists in Seattle, Washington, which was most inconvienent, especially when someone wanted a pictorial poster in a hurry.

Finally, the proper artist was found almost on our own doorstep, in the person of Herb Ashley, of Banff, Alberta, a part-time commercial artist with an understanding flair for show posters. The speed with which he could dash off top-notch drawings was remarkable.

The type-high blank boards we used came from the United States and were made of basswood, one sheet size. Basswood had been found the most suitable for this work because of its toughness and soft, close grain. Using other woods such as spruce, with a hard grain, would result in the grain pattern showing in the printing. The boards were planed to exactly the height of printing type and smoothly surfaced on one side for engraving.

We tried our first efforts on wood block engravings on the folk near home by producing a series of posters for sports days, picturing baseball players, horse races, athletic events, humorous scenes and so on. These were half sheets with the pictorial design covering the top half of the poster and were printed up in quantity and stored on shelves.

As orders came in, the wording supplied for local events

was printed in the blank space at the bottom. All type material used for this, including spacing, type lines, etc., was standardized to fit this space.

There was enough uniformity in sports day poster copy even from different far-apart towns, that a skilled compositor and one pressman produced as many as a dozen orders in a day (one every 40 minutes), all the result of standardization and mass production. The order for each usually ran from 50 to 150 copies.

Most printers would say that such a feat is impossible. Certainly the average country printing office with its limited variety of type faces and an unsuitable press would be fortunate to turn out one order of half-sheet posters in half a day.

Most of this business came in May and June so again it was an easy forward step to set up a similar service for summer fairs which began in July and continuing until the end of August.

By this time, we were sufficiently experienced to take on carnival and circus work, as well as theatrical billboard posters up to 24 sheets in size, with dimensions of 21 feet long and nine feet high.

One of our best customers in the circus field was Clyde Beatty who, while in Canada, would buy liberal quantities of pictorial paper and carry it south on his train when he returned to the United States.

As always, one had to expect from time to time problems of a most unusual nature.

One of these was in connection with the order for pictorial posters of various sizes for the Australian National Band which was making a tour of Western Canada fairs and portions of the United States.

It was requested in general terms that the Southern Cross constellation (as important to those "down under" as the Big Dipper is to Canadians) be shown on the posters.

A glance at some Australian postage stamps showed two formations of the cross. The Winnipeg Public Library came up with seven different pictures of it, each as viewed from widely separated locations at different times of the year.

Which one did the band management want? There was

no air mail then, and enquiry by mail via steamship would have taken six weeks. There was of course cable communication but those were the days before pictures could be sent by wire. So we just used the one which appeared the most balanced and artistic. There were no complaints.

When the order and instructions came for Royal Air Force Band posters, it was specified with military precision and firmness that the uniforms of the pictured bandsmen must be the exact shade of blue-grey as the uniforms they wore.

It would have been a very simple request to comply with, had a swatch of the proper cloth accompanied the order. But that latter important item was missing.

Enquiries were made over a fair-sized area with the object of locating a former RAF serviceman, but with no success.

All we could learn was that the shade of color used in the uniforms of Royal Air Force was not the same as that used by Royal Canadian Air Force.

A query was made at Ottawa, but no one there could come up with a sample of the cloth or anything else that would show the proper color. England was three to four weeks away by mail and enquiry there would have delayed the production of the posters beyond the stipulated delivery date.

The situation seemed hopeless. But again a "doorstep miracle" resolved it.

On mentioning our trouble to a Rouleau storekeeper, he at once told of an RAF man working on a farm about six miles from town. I phoned this man, told him my story, and was assured he would come to see me in a couple of days as he felt he could be of some help.

He arrived two days later, but his first comment was somewhat disappointing. He had no RAF uniform. He suggested that if we had different colors of inks he felt he could correctly pick out the correct shade.

This resulted in the mixing of inks in different shades of blue, with white and black added. After several mixes he finally said, "I am sure that is it"—indicating the mixture last compounded.

We had only his word that the color he had chosen was correct, and there was no way to confirm his opinion. So we went ahead with the color he selected, and hoped for the best.

His sense of color proved to be fantastic. Later, it was most gratifying to watch members of the band, when it came to Regina, walking past the full-sized pictures on billboard posters. The color of their uniforms and that on the posters were absolutely identical.

Man, regardless of how humble he might be or of how high a rank he has reached in life, interests me. There's something to learn from all of them.

—SAM J. LATTA, Govan, Sask., *Prairie News.*

Chapter 13

A GOLDEN ERA

The golden era of the legitimate theatrical stage on the western prairies began in the early 1890s when a few companies came in from the United States to appear in public halls in Winnipeg.

With the building of branch railway lines on which towns with a population of a few hundred people grew up, more of the smaller companies entered from south of the border, bringing entertainment sorely needed to add a diversion to the routine pace of daily life, with even the odd bit of cultural stimulation added.

These companies presented every type of stage entertainment.

It was a time when melodrama would rouse audiences to cheer the rescue of the young maiden from the clutches of the leering, black-moustached villain.

"East Lynne," with all its wholesome pleasantries and "Uncle Tom's Cabin" with its gamut of warm emotion, sadness, passion and drama, were played over and over again.

There were comedies with clean humor that old and young might enjoy; black-faced minstrels with their interlocutor and endmen, bones and tambourines, sparkling with snappy wit, glorious male voices and specialty acts; magicians, hypnotists, elocutionists and medicine shows.

The technique of stage performance was less artificial in those days. Performers did not need to adopt mannerisms to win applause, but if they lacked genuine talent they were more likely to be booed.

The Canadian prairie country became exclusive territory for American companies to play, and to this day, remains almost wholly dominated by American producers of indoor and outdoor commercialized amusement. This situation is due to the unpopulated miles stretching eastward and westward from its borders.

About 1910, the number of shows playing the west began to increase noticeably, and this continued until the coming of the first silent movies. Theatre facilities were provided mainly by retail store owners, who would build a stage on the second floor of their premises and put in kitchen chairs for seating with maybe a few plank seats in the rear. In rare cases, municipal buildings were the public halls.

With the growth of population of prairie cities, two men became prominent in the theatrical field.

These were C. P. Walker, of Winnipeg, Manitoba, and W. B. Sherman who at different times made his home in Calgary, Alberta and Moose Jaw and Regina, Saskatchewan.

In many ways the personalities of these two men were in marked contrast.

Mr. Walker was a man of great integrity, and a gentleman highly respected. He keenly felt a responsibility to provide his patrons with the finest of entertainment possible to secure.

He was known throughout Canada as one of the most discriminating in choice of attractions booked into his theatre and over his circuit.

Without a doubt, William B. Sherman was the most bizarre individual ever engaged in the theatrical business in the Canadian west. He first came to Canada from the United States on a vaudeville circuit with his own animal act, which consisted of one educated goat! Sherman was not, by any means, a headliner with this act. He gained recognition in Canada in an entirely different phase of the business. He parted with the goat and turned to operating theatres and producing his own shows, both drama and musical.

At one time he simultaneously operated a theatre in each of four cities, playing road shows as well as his own small musical comedy companies.

His first venture was management of the Grand Theatre in Calgary, built by a local group of investors.

Bill was an uncouth man with only a meagre education.

He was heavily built with a substantial girth. Though attired in the best styled clothing, it always seemed to clash with his personality. His voice was rough and coarse, yet such irritation was forgotten through the cleverness he displayed in business negotiations.

In his most prosperous times he loaded his person with diamonds. There were diamonds outlining his initials on the back of his big watch; diamonds on cuff links, locket, rings and tie pin; rings of diamonds around his fountain pen and cigar holder.

He had a ritual when it came to paying a dinner check. At least three rolls of money would be drawn from different pockets, the first usually made up of $100 bills. All of them would be at least partially leafed through, and he did not hesitate to let it be known that he carried a loaded revolver.

The opening of the Grand Theatre was an exciting social event with the cream of the city's society in the box seats and parquet.

A British company presenting Dickens' plays had been engaged for a week's stand as being most in keeping with the cultural atmosphere of the gala affair, and with the appointments of the finest theatre on the prairies.

There was one jarring note in the harmony of the decor of its interior. Bill had sold advertising space on the stage fire curtain to different businessmen with the wording of each painted in the most garish fashion and colors, which clashed with the graceful proscenium and its artistic tinting.

City newspapers of the morning following the first performance praised the stage presentation but scorned the advertising curtain.

Bill's feelings were hurt. The second night during the first intermission, he suddenly appeared in front of the curtain attired in a rented full dress suit, which did not fit his ungainly body any too well. The coat was skimpy, with a white vest adding prominence to his expansive midriff.

He began: "Ladies and gentlesmen. Youse have no doubt seen in the papers somthin' about this here curtain." He jerked one thumb backward to the item referred to and continued, "I ask youse what is the matter with that there curtain?"

By this time the subdued chuckling broke into a roar of laughter. The contrast of his manner of speech with the perfect English spoken by the actors had its effect.

Bill began to perspire. He awkwardly reached into a hip pocket and brought out a bright red hankerchief—a cotton one of the kind used by the laboring men of the times. As he mopped his face and neck with this it became a comedy bit that had the entire audience convulsed. Had he deliberately planned the routine he could never have written a more effective script.

Poor Bill attempted to make himself heard once more, but without success. His justifications of the advertising curtain were never heard. He quickly slipped backstage.

W. B. Sherman died a poor man. With the coming of moving pictures, he was unable or unwilling to adjust to the new type of entertainment. The live stage talent which he used so profitably, disappeared, and with its departure went the source of his income.

In the final days of his long life he sold miscellaneous wares from a push cart on the streets of Vancouver.

No one knows the number of actors or actresses who reached stardom after serving an apprenticeship with companies touring the Canadian west, but two stand out prominently.

One was Boris Karloff, the horror film star, whose real name was William Henry Pratt. As a young Englishman who tried several different occupations after arrival in Canada, he finally joined the Harry St. Clair Stock Company while it was playing Kamloops, B.C.

I met him when the company was playing Rouleau and found him a gentle, courteous young man, so different from the monsters he later portrayed on stage and screen. He was alert, keen-minded, with an inquisitiveness about everything and everyone he came in contact with.

The other was Miss Verna Felton, who in the early 1920s had her name in lights on Broadway, New York, latterly moving to Hollywood where she played prominent parts in TV movie serials.

The three western provinces can also lay claim to being the area over which Gerald A. Moore—later acclaimed the world's greatest piano accompanist—travelled his first professional engagement in that role. In the year 1915, at the age of 16 he accepted the invitation from Boris Hambourg, 'cellist and Redfern Hollinshead, tenor, to be their accompanist on a tour of the Canadian west. Clad in an Eton suit, he was billed as "The Remarkable English Boy Pianist." He was paid $40, plus hotel and travelling expenses, for forty appearances—certainly a vivid contrast to the several hundred dollars he regularly received for one night engagements a decade later.

At the age of 20 he returned to England and in a short time began to accompany virtually every singer of note in Britain and all European countries.

One had rare experiences in dealing with owners of circuses and carnivals and other outdoor shows. As a group, their personalities were much different from those connected with the legitimate theatre as producers of drama, comedy, opera and other forms of cultural art.

To be successful, everyone connected with the production and management of any type of public entertainment has to be a keen assessor of public preferences, changing likes and dislikes and timeliness of presentations as well as having a keen business sense. But none face the array of complexities which confront the circus and carnival owner who must have a unique temperament, coupled with the ability to make quick decisions to cope with problems that keep coming up every day.

A circus may be looked upon as a small community that differs from all others simply because it is constantly on the move.

But it is an unusual type of community populated by people with unusual talents and requirements. There are performers, workmen, side show people, concessionaires, musicians, truck drivers, electricians, mechanics, office help, public relations men and even hangers-on, who until recent

years could lose themselves for a while in a constantly perin-
grinating group of maybe several hundred persons.

Then, as if this motley collection did not furnish enough
distraction, governments have added their bits with electrical,
safety, health and sanitation inspectors; education, sales and
income tax, pension and unemployment insurance assessment,
provincial taxes and local license collectors.

Yet, with all this kind of daily stress, circus and carnival
owners were and are, on contact, rarely other than robust,
smiling and aggressive gentlemen.

Doing business with these folk produced some unusual
experiences.

This could be expected. All were top men in their respective fields. All sparkled with a flair for showmanship
which brought them success over the years, yet each with a
slightly different personality.

With some, showmanship had become so much a part of
their nature, it was always present. With others it would
become evident through occasional spontaneous acts from
which they drew their own satisfaction and amusement.
Like that of Patty Conklin, when he paid the substantial
balance owing on his season's printing account entirely in
silver coinage. I had only to catch the twinkle in his eye to
know that he would derive the greatest pleasure from the
stunt if I went along with it in a dumb manner.

As his cashier pushed out the big stack of rolled coins,
I began, one at a time, to put them in different pockets,
while he made a casual excuse that his partner had just taken
all the folding money down to the railway station to pay for
his train move to the next location.

By the time I had all the money stowed away it felt that
the breaking of a single stitch in each pocket would result in
the entire load cascading to the floor. The total weight was
around 35 pounds.

The secondary pleasure I received later was from the
look that appeared on the face of the bank teller as I kept
taking roll after roll out of my pockets and shoving them
through his wicket. The climax was reached when he burst
out in language probably never before heard from his side

of the counter, in the dignified and restrained atmosphere of a bank, with the words "where in hell did you get all that?"

Then, there was Floyd King of King Bros. Circus, who at Vancouver, B.C., cleaned up the hefty balance of his season's account with bundles of paper money. The settlement was made late at night following a second show. He said he would reduce the risk of my being noticed and robbed on my way from the circus lot to my hotel. He wrapped the money in a newspaper and tied it with binder twine, (I have often wondered where he picked up that item). The parcel did look like one containing four pounds of butter such as farmers delivered to city customers, rather than one containing paper currency.

Possibly one of the most unusual settlements of an account we ever received was through the passing of a special bill by a provincial government authorizing a special grant to a bankrupt fair board in sufficient amount to pay the Enterprise Show Print account which had been overlooked in setting up the amount of a previous grant.

As the settlement of circus and carnival accounts were most often in goodly amounts and almost always in cash, the counting of the money could take up considerable time.

I soon discovered that there was no need to check the amount of currency handed to me, usually in bundles of $100 and $500, and would take it to the bank without checking each bundle. Never once during the operation of Enterprise Show Print or King Show Print did the banks find a shortage of even one dollar in the money so deposited.

The end of the theatrical era on the prairies coincided with the final years of Second World War.

The last of the road shows was the Richard Kent Stock Company which for several years played almost continuously, other than for holiday breaks, on a circuit of one-night stands during which it visited from 60 to 70 different towns.

Dick Kent was an actor of the old school with a versatility in portraying different roles. He had been a star with several of the finest repertory companies playing the largest cities in the United States.

The members of his cast were most capable players

so that his presentations were of a much higher standard than those produced by most companies playing previously to small town audiences. But movies were drawing more and more people away from stage shows. Lack of patrons finally forced Dick to disband his company. It was a sad ending, almost pitiable, for a man who had previously held such a high position on the American stage.

While playing in Chicago where his name shone every night in bright lights on the front of the theatre where he played, success had built up his ego and his independent spirit.

"I was to blame entirely," he told me, "for giving up my career in that city, then forming my own company and heading for the vast countryside. I thought I could make a mint of money playing the smaller cities with royalty plays, little realizing that most people had never heard of me and that stage dramas and comedies were losing out to the new attractions of motion pictures."

After playing some of the central states he had brought his company to Canada as the growing number of movie houses kept pressuring him to seek more profitable territory.

So it can be said that Richard Kent was the last talented actor to play the western Canadian provinces as the legitimate stage faded into memory.

Chapter 14

CHAUTAUQUAS

To Canadians born after 1930, the name "Chautauqua" will mean very little; yet for ten to fifteen years previous to that date the Chautauqua was a commercialized movement bringing to the smaller towns of the western prairies pleasing entertainment of a high standard, with a degree of "culture" placing it in a distinctive role.

Chautauqua began as an attempt at adult education with headquarters at a lake of the same name in the state of New York. It actually was an outgrowth of Methodist camp meetings, when the teaching of secular subjects, handicrafts and even some technical subjects was introduced. Then came the bringing in of the most noted orators of the nation, providing the topics they discussed were not controversial but stimulated moral and intellectual uplift.

A short time later, promoters in the entertainment field recognized the possibilities of profit through presenting very much the same type of program over ten- or twelve-week circuits throughout the United States and Canada.

The Dominion Chautauquas, operated by J. M. Erickson out of Calgary, concentrated on summer circuits for which tents were used. There was not a town played which had a public hall large enough to seat more than a portion of the crowds which turned out for the performances. For a whole week Chautauqua became the absorbing interest of the townsfolk, with performances each afternoon and night.

Usually the afternoon program featured a lecturer. For the evening there would be instrumental or vocal numbers, elocutionists, and sometimes a good dramatic company presenting a wholesome play.

Only season tickets were sold for the 12 programs so that rarely were the audiences less than capacity, even though the people had to endure the discomfort of sitting on hard plank seats, and in stifling temperatures at times.

The promotion was skilfully organized. To secure a Chautauqua, a group of local people had to guarantee payment of the fee set by the company. The signers had then to see that enough season tickets were sold to cover the guarantee, or foot any deficit themselves. They had to take care of all the local preparatory work and advertising promotion.

A well-versed superintendent arrived in town a day ahead of the opening and then acted as master of ceremonies for the week. This was always a personable young woman, capable of smoothing out any little bit of friction that might arise. Her final task was to catch the enthusiasm at its peak, and secure enough signatures to the contract that would bring Chautauqua back again the next year.

For many years, one impressario, Wallace Graham of Toronto had booked small groups of outstanding Canadian musicians and entertainers into nearly every town in Saskatchewan and Alberta. Headliners among these were Jimmy Fax, comedian; Maude Buschlen, violinist; Ruthven Macdonald, basso; Arlene Jackson, comedienne; Jessie MacLachlan, Scottish soprano; Mark Hambourg, pianist and Boris Hambourg, 'cellist, and the Swiss Bell Ringers.

Nearly every one of these companies had their printing done by Enterprise Show Print. It was intriguing to have to deal with the peculiar notions some had as to the style of posters and other printing they used.

Boris Hambourg insisted that his programs be printed on soft paper. He had good point. While the practice had disappeared of shelling peanuts and eating them with gusto while listening to vocalists and instrumentalists perform, Boris had found that the handling by his audiences of programs printed on crackly paper was an irritating accompaniment to the softer passages of the selections he played.

Graham became fascinated with Chautauqua, and was anxious to promote one that would play three days in each town in town halls during the fall season, but he lacked the necessary financial backing.

The idea had appeal. The head office would be set up in Rouleau and of course all the printing would be done by Enterprise Show Print. It would be of a style entirely different from the bold, glaring posters used by theatrical road shows, circuses and carnivals. It had to have "class," requiring fine glossy paper, art work, halftones with the finest of screens, and the use of the best of black and colored inks.

Only a small addition to the plant was required to make it capable of producing the high standard of printing required, and members of the staff had the necessary skill.

In 1925, a company was organized with a Dominion charter under the name of Community Chautauquas Limited. There were seven shareholders, six being local Rouleau people along with Graham.

The circuit had first to be booked and this presented a problem. What sort of price should be stipulated in the contract? The company had no experience in the business to provide data on various costs involved.

Yet with Graham's knowledge of talent cost and with a great deal of calculation covering train transportation, booking, office overhead, printing, telephones, telegrams, postage, and those multitudinous items which are grouped as general expense, plus the expert advice of a banker and shareholder, J. W. Paul, a final figure was determined.

Yet apprehension remained. Was it sufficient to provide the company with an over-all profit at the end of the season?

It was. Community Chautauquas was the only one of the many set up on the North American continent to show a profit on its first year of operation.

Graham had no trouble booking one 10-week circuit or engaging his talent and superintendents and setting up his programs. The second year two circuits were booked.

It was Community Chautauquas which first introduced Agnes Macphail, Canada's first woman member of parliament, to the Chautauqua field. While it had been a long-standing policy of all Chautauqua companies to refrain from engaging lecturers who were prominent in national politics, Graham recognized that Miss Macphail had established a reputation as a colorful and unique public speaker who could fluently and expertly discuss many current public problems involving the farming industry, education, international relationships, prison reform, all with a new outlook, and with deep sincerity. There was more than a mere touch of showmanship in her manner of making quick and cutting retorts when heckled in Parliament or public meeting.

It was on the Community Chautauqua circuit that she created a story given considerable prominence by the press of the day.

While Miss Macphail was speaking, a man in the front row of seats kept saying, "Aw, why don't you get a husband." For a while she ignored these interruptions. Then pointing at him, she walked to the front of the platform and told him to "get up!" It was only after she repeated the command, which the audience echoed that the man got up awkwardly and stood there.

"I suppose you're married," said Agnes.

He mumbled agreement.

Then she spoke to the audience: "Now, I'd bet he wasn't like this when his wife married him 10 years ago."

Pointing her finger again at the man, she said: "What guarantee have I that anybody I married now wouldn't turn out like you in 10 years?"

It was the sort of repartee which audiences enjoyed immensely.

Miss MacPhail was paid $100 per week, the salary usually paid lecturers on prairie circuits. A few received $125.

She enjoyed her tour very much and with the feeling she was reaching people wholly unfamiliar with her crusade against social and economic injustices in Canada, particularly those involving agriculture and rural life.

One phase of her engagement she did not like. It was the strict rule among show people that the first train had to be taken out of town after each performance. This meant that regular hours for sleep and relaxation were the exception rather than the rule.

It was following Miss Macphail's break-in with Community

Chautauquas that she became well-known as a lecturer in the United States, being booked by entertainment bureaus for special appearances at conventions and group gatherings.

Another lady lecturer with Community Chautauquas was Senator Belle Kearney of Louisiana. She had the warmth of personality common to so many people of the deep south, together with a keen appreciation of wholesome humor. These characteristics did not detract from the aura of dignity which she possessed, but rather added to its charm.

She was an experienced trouper, having appeared on several Chautauqua circuits throughout the coastal states, but it was her first trip to Canada. In that respect she was a real tenderfoot, particularly during the colder days of late autumn during the last few weeks of the circuit.

However, it did not take her long to learn that when a steam heated room became chilly, extra heat could usually be secured by opening the valve on the steam coil. This elementary piece of knowledge on one occasion got her into trouble.

It was a cold windy day when Community Chautauquas opened at Melville. She arrived along with the other talent just in time to get a lunch before going to the town hall to deliver her lecture on the afternoon program. She found her hotel room quite chilly, so before leaving it she turned the steam valve open to its very limit.

Three hours later she returned happy with the prospect she would find the room warm and comfortable. Unlocking its door and opening it she was greeted with a dense burst of steam. She instantly reacted to the thought that the valve must be shut off, and quickly.

Dashing into the mass of blinding steam, her feet went from under her and she fell on the linoleum covered floor. Helpless, her momentum carried her along the slippery surface until she struck the corner of the washstand, just at the right angle to upset it along with its wash basin and water pitcher. They crashed to the floor, breaking into several pieces to complete the ruination of everything in the room.

The finish of every piece of furniture was ruined; the wall paper on walls and ceiling hung in shreds; her baggage was thoroughly soaked. In brief, it was all a complete mess.

But Senator Belle Kearney was not one to claim that the damage resulted from an act of God. It was the result of her inexperience as a tenderfoot and she was prepared to pay for it, which indeed she did, in spite of the hotel owner's first insistence that the incident was one of the expected risks in operating a public stopping place.

The majority of artists engaged by Wallace Graham were Canadians, mostly from eastern Canada. He felt this would help build a bridge between the east and the west, creating a better understanding between people of widely separated areas.

Yet he did not ignore western talent. One of his finest soloists was a Saskatchewan boy named Henry Ardill, who had a beautiful tenor voice, which top critics in eastern Canada simply raved about.

Then there was Walter McRaye of Vancouver, who for many years starred with Pauline Johnson, the famous Indian poetess on her tours. He was with her when she went to England in 1906 under the patronage of Lord and Lady Strathcona, and he added greatly to Canadian interest by his inimitable rendering of Dr. Drummond's "Habitant" poems. They made a second tour to England the next year and on return engaged with an American Chautauqua for the summer season. They continued to present programs together until Miss Johnson's health failed.

Mr. McRaye, in keeping with his talent, was a headliner on Community Chautauquas Ltd. programs.

In 1929, Chautauqua had begun to lose its charm, mainly for the reason that local people became tired of selling tickets, the work of putting up tents of the summer Chautauqua, and all the many little chores involved, and then finally handing all the receipts over to the company—with maybe a little more if the ticket sales were not up to the mark. In addition, the shades of the coming depression had begun to fall, with money becoming a bit tighter.

Little criticism was ever expressed as to the merit of the programs presented.

Community Chautauquas in 1929 sold all its contracts for

1930 to Dominion Chautauquas, and Enterprise Show Print lost a fine customer. By 1931, Dominion also went out of business. The "dirty thirties" made it quite definite that the bare necessities of life took high precedence over entertainment.

> When divorces are as common as tumbling weeds hung up on barb wire fences, it is nice to know there are men and women who have lived together for 60 years and are only anxious to go right on living together.
>
> —W. J. REDMOND in *Rags and Tatters*,
> *Maple Creek News*.

Chapter 15

LOCAL NEWS HIGHLIGHTS

The operation of a country newspaper was a somewhat prosaic task. The *Rouleau Enterprise* was typical of the average weekly.

The news of the community followed a rather even tenor. There were such routine matters to report as rural and town council meetings, weather and crop conditions (a feature that non-resident subscribers, mostly landowners, appreciated), baseball games in summer and hockey and curling in the winter, church and school activities, election of lodge officers, local elections, club meetings, social gatherings, births, marriages and deaths and a column or two of short paragraphs recording the coming and going of individuals.

In the early years, it was not uncommon to have birth notices in a weekly newspaper accepted as proof of age of the person concerned. Such reference was only necessary in cases of those born before the more rigid birth registration regulations of the new province were effectively enforced.

Yet in all the reporting of such everyday events was recorded the history of each community. There remains no other source of information revealing the broad image of the overall way of life of its people as well as trends in the areas of politics, economies and society.

Even advertisements, in their own style—modest and polite as compared with those of modern times—reflected buying habits and prices for all sorts of commodities in daily use, such as farm implements, washing machines, building materials, groceries, clothing, or even toys and children's games.

It is unfortunate that many of the early files of weekly

newspapers have disappeared, some destroyed by fire, some simply neglected and lost. All contained from time to time, bits of history that someone, sometime, may be searching for.

It was with this in mind, that the government of Saskatchewan some years ago, started a worthy task—the microfilming of all available copies of weekly newspapers and filing these in the provincial archives.

Occasionally there would be a news highlight.

There was the visit to Rouleau of Lord Byng, then Governor General of Canada. It was one of the very few visits he made to small centers during his conscientious search for knowledge of the economic and social background of the land and its inhabitants. It was a trip which took him to widely separated parts of the Dominion—to desolate Arctic regions as well as to crowded urban centers.

He came to watch nine binders drawn by tractors taking successive swaths to mow down the ripe wheat crop of a 160-acre field on a six-section farm. It was a rare sight, a forecast of the development of large-scale power farming on the prairies.

First there was the official welcome in town with decorated platform, be-medalled veterans who had fought proudly under his command in Europe, school children in rigid rows, an encircling crowd, band music, introductions and brief speeches. Somehow it seemed to stir a deeper pride in all things Canadian. It made a rare story.

Of course, much of the material published could be considered trivial in the minds of historians, yet these items mirrored clearly the characteristics of the people creating the social atmosphere of the community.

For example, one could find in the columns of *The Rouleau Enterprise* stories of the annual Sunday church parade of the members of the local Masonic lodge. (All secret societies kept their names in the public eye by attending one church service each year.) But the Masonic brethren outshone all others. Their parade had an aristocractic touch, reminiscent of British ceremonial.

Each was attired in a black frock coat, black trousers,

black shoes and a high silk hat, more commonly known to the rank and file as a "plug" hat.

The march from lodge room to church and return was quite impressive. It would have made a nice little news movie. The absence of a band with only the muffled sound of marching feet on the surface of the dirt street added a dignity to it all.

The parade of the Loyal Order of Orangemen on the 12th of July was much in contrast. Led by "King William" in full uniform, riding a horse, with drums stoutly beaten and piccolos playing "The Protestant Boy" and other appropriate tunes, there was the strong impression of a militant religious faith.

Reports of such parades, together with a summary of the sermons extolling the virtues of the various rituals of the orders found a place in the news columns. A particularly eloquent sermon was sometimes printed in pamphlet form to bring another job to the printer.

The advent of the First World War began a change in the outlook, purpose and well-being of weekly newspapers.

As the years of war lengthened, interest in the national effort became more intense. Greater emphasis was given to stories of the nation's military activities. Much of this was in the form of War Department releases, but the local scene was not neglected.

In this respect the weekly newspapers proved their value in penetrating to even the remotest corners of their communities. The information disseminated through this channel proved of great assistance in promoting various phases of the war effort.

One of the most timely and important tasks was in connection with the Victory Bond campaigns. Few people in rural areas at that time had any idea of what a bond really was. The average man considered bonds as a form of investment exclusively for the wealthy.

The initial campaign in the form of news stories, editorials and advertisements promoted an entirely new concept of investment. It made people conscious that money was needed to carry on the war—their money. It made them aware that a government bond could be bought for a comparatively few dollars, and interest would be paid to the purchaser each year, and that at the end of a stated period of years the original amount invested would be returned. All of which was a basic lesson in practical economics.

Quite naturally, the appeal to people to buy Victory Bonds included that of patriotism. This in the earlier promotions of bond issues had almost as much persuasive influence in making sales as that of interest return on money invested.

In fact, there were those who never absorbed the elementary lesson in its full import but purchased bonds with an understanding on their part that the money they parted with was nothing more than a gift to the government in financial need.

This fact never came to light until canvassers went out to sell bonds again during the Second World War. Then they found in the possession of various individuals, bonds issued during the first war with every interest coupon still attached. The owners appeared surprised that these could be clipped off and cashed at any bank for the sum stated on each.

The success resulting from advertising bond issues in weekly newspapers redounded to the benefit of the latter. Governments, provincial and federal, became aware of the efficiency of the weeklies as a medium through which the rural population could be most fully and conveniently contacted.

As the years went by, more and more government departments used them in publicizing matters of immediate importance.

The First World War produced a heavy financial burden on the entire nation. The borrowing of money to meet the cost of the war produced a debt of a size previously undreamed of.

This situation initiated the personal income tax. The first announcement of it suggested that it might be only temporary. The tax rate was very low at the time and only a few persons were in the assessable class. Those with normal average incomes were not even aware of its rather quiet and painless entry into Canada's taxation program. It has become the outstanding example of the principle that a tax once applied is rarely, if ever, removed.

The impact of the costs of the war had begun to build up a relentless pressure on all phases of national life. This was to continue through the depression years of the '30s to become a backlog on which the troubles of the Second World War were subsequently added.

The entire outlook of national existence was changing. The nation was in a disturbed state of mind. The old conventional props were gone. Yet it seemed that the skilful organization of the armed forces, so necessary in winning the war, had added something new to the thinking of all Canadians.

Group organization seemed to provide answers to many personal troubles that began to appear. New groups with specific objectives were being formed such as the Canadian Legion, Saskatchewan Farmers' Union, The United Grain Growers, and many with purely local significance.

While this newly evident spirit of co-operation did not provide the original initiative in the church union movement involving Methodist, Presbyterian and Congregational churches in Canada, it had its influence in hastening the consummation of the proceedings throughout the prairies.

The Rouleau Presbyterian and Methodist churches had reached an agreement in 1921, by setting up their own basis of union two years before the three parent bodies in Canada brought their negotiations to a successful conclusion.

This local union became more than handwriting on a bit of paper and an intermingling of souls. The Presbyterian Church building was moved and attached to the Methodist one. The contents of the corner stones of both were removed and replaced in a new cornerstone together with current mementoes which in years to come would again be uncovered to reveal appropriate bits of history of the past.

However, one custom remained that seemed at odds with the success of the union. The former Methodists still sat in their opera-like individual seats in the front portion of the church which was their original building. The former Pres-

byterians appropriately stayed with their unyielding solid
oak pews in their original building. But both were quite
content. A new modern edifice has definitely wiped out any
indication of non-co-operation.

All of this produced another of the few appealing stories
in the lifetime of *The Rouleau Enterprise.*

Yet in the midst of a dirth of noteworthy stories, I failed
to recognize the first quiet murmurings of an event which
became the biggest story of all—one that is now known back
and forth and up and down the North American continent.

It was the shaping up of one of the most colorful bits of
Saskatchewan history—the establishment of Notre Dame
College at Wilcox (10 miles from Rouleau), by Father Athol
Murray.

The College was the outcome of Father Murray's deep
interest in underprivileged boys, first manifest while he was
serving as Chancellor for Archbishop Mathieu of Regina,
when he founded an athletic club.

Following the death of the Archbishop, he was offered a
choice of parishes. He chose Wilcox. Several of the boys
followed him there. These, together with others with little or
no means, but craving a high school education, eventually
filled every nook and corner, basement to attic, of the rectory.

He arranged with the nuns of the local Convent to teach
the boys.

The thought of providing still higher education for them
grew in Father Murray's mind. But to do that he would need
a college.

I can recall him presenting the subject to me. I mumbled
around a bit, saying something about the lack of appropriate
surroundings. It did not seem practical that a college should
be located in a little isolated village made up of a few store
buildings and plain houses built of lumber without any regard
for architectural beauty, the whole sitting in loneliness on a
flat plain with faraway horizons.

Rather, a college should be built of brick and stone,
half hidden by trees and approached by curving avenues
bordered with stately elms.

Only a few months ago Monsiegneur Athol Murray

wrote to me saying "Andy, we now have the trees." He had remembered what I had forgotten.

Now Notre Dame has more than trees. It has a faculty of 17, approximately 300 students—Canadians, Americans, Chinese, Philippinos and Nigerians—and buildings valued at more than three million dollars, including a skating rink with the largest sheet of skating ice on the continent, size 90 by 200 feet.

A 55-foot stone structure, named the Tower of God, contains symbols and relics of the Christian, Hebrew and Muslim faiths. If located in a large city it would attract thousands of viewers every year.

I now know that I carelessly missed recording the beginning of this rare story by failing to recognize Father Athol Murray's capacity and determination to make a dream come true, and his firm belief in the power of prayer.

Chapter 16

CHAIN WEEKLIES

Newspapermen have had the reputation of being non-conformists, but in the weekly newspaper field they have been for the most, conformists. They have tended to promote the ideas of others for community betterment, rather than ideas of their own, although they have, as a rule, been quite selective in accepting the ideas of others.

Compared with present-day metropolitan newspaper standards, nearly all of the earlier weekly newspaper editors were tolerant men, with no leanings toward sensationalism, insofar as news reporting was concerned.

Maybe this was in great part due to the fact that most editors were printers first and writers last, lacking in skill and imagination in making news stories more colorful and interesting.

The time element also affected the situation. With a limited gross dollar volume of business, the printing staffs had to be kept at a minimum size, requiring the average newspaper owner to spend much of his time in his printing plant—a duty not conducive to the stimulation of literary effort.

The result was that few aimed to present more than a recording of each week's local events. In addition, there was a general adherence to a policy that any local incident reflecting on anyone's character in any way was not reported.

If all the unpublished stories stored in the memories of weekly newspaper editors were to be printed, many books would be required to contain them.

They would picture the whole gamut of human emotions. Each would be sparked in a different manner—by a touch

of drama, a bit of rare sentiment, some droll humor or wit-
ticism and even tomfoolery on the part of those involved.

There would be the intriguing story held in complete
secrecy because of a confidence bestowed on the recipient,
maybe by a politician who had later found by a turn of events
that all his planning and scheming had come to naught.

Or a bit of scandal which had unwittingly been uncovered;
or a depressing tale of unattained ambition; or the aftermath
of a heart-rending sorrow suffered by an individual or a
family.

There were good reasons why many of these tales were
never printed, and rarely related, even to a small circle of
close acquaintances.

Contained in the rule book of nearly every editor and
weekly publisher was the policy that personal feelings of all
other individuals must be considered and good taste observed
in reporting at all times.

The weekly newspaper business was considered as one
carrying sober responsibilities of which the most important
was accurate reporting of local activities, along with sedate
and friendly recording of the social affairs within its sphere.
It had no space for sensational writing, particularly that
which was frivolous or hurtful to anyone.

This sympathetic and friendly approach mirrored the
cameraderie prevalent among the people of smaller communities, where everyone knew everyone else, their virtues and
their failings—a wholesome and enriching experience, now
so much lacking where greater density of population breeds
frustrations and disregard for others' rights.

In addition to the coverage of the more important
happenings, every weekly newspaper carried a column headed
"Local Notes" or equivalent designation. Here were to be
found such items as "Mrs. John Jones entertained several
friends to tea on Wednesday afternoon," or "Mr. Phil
Thorneycroft left on Tuesday, on a business trip to Winnipeg."
The same type of references to personal activities were to be
found in the country correspondent's writings, coming from
settlements in the rural areas nearby.

These items were just as much the lifeblood of the

newspaper as any other feature, in spite of their apparent superficiality. Not only did people like to see their names in print (as they still do in connection with worthy cause or effort) but these bits of trivia had a place in sustaining personal acquaintanceship when distance was a barrier, and other means of communication non-existent.

The sophisticated society page of today's daily newspaper is the offspring of this early column of neighborly news.

Before the turn of the century, a goodly proportion of towns had two newspapers but to a much lesser degree in Saskatchewan and Alberta than in Manitoba.

Editorials were rarely written by country editors except in towns where there were two newspapers.

Yet in actual fact, the bulk of subscriptions to local weekly newspapers were not sold primarilly because of the presence of editorial columns, but because of good news coverage. The latter is the more important from the reader's viewpoint. Editorials became a secondary feature, yet one which does add prestige to the more basic service it is expected to render, especially when such writings are based on sound concepts and clearly expressed.

After the turn of the century, most communities were served by only one weekly newspaper. The emphasis on politics began to disappear. Then with the advent of the First World War, there was born a new outlook on national unity with an atmosphere of greater responsibility in presenting sane leadership and more tempered opinion.

Dozens of printing plants were put into operation in the new towns which sprang up and grew like mushrooms. Many were subsidized in one way or another by the businessmen, even to liberal guarantee of advertising patronage. Every town or even village of any size felt it must have a newspaper.

Before the first 25 years of this century had passed, the weekly newspapers of the prairies had reached an over-all standard of merit that brought well-deserved recognition and established them firmly as a most essential business contributing to community service and welfare.

In addition, the economic changes which had eliminated

many had stopped the growth or even made ghost places of the smaller towns and villages.

While the smaller places were gradually fading away and losing their printing offices and newspapers, a new type of weekly appeared. These were printed and issued by outside offices that were sometimes one hundred miles distant from the area they served. They were accepted as providing an advertising service as well as bolstering local pride and morale.

This type of newspaper was most prevalent in Saskatchewan where as many as 38 offices have participated at one time or another in printing and publishing them. Only a few were ever started in Manitoba or Alberta. Their history provides a story combining hopeful promotion, earnest effort, partial success, frenzied finance and sometimes bankruptcy.

The one person most prominent in this specialty field was Father James Branch, a priest at Gravelbourg, Sask. Along with his parish work he was active in the Boy Scout movement and conceived the idea of a publication for the Scouts.

Gathering some printing equipment, he made a printing course part of Scout work. This met with some success, and he saw the possibility, with the plant and the boys he trained, to become publisher of weekly news media for towns in the area that wanted such service. His establishment became known as the Model Print Shop.

He met with some success, and in order to be more centrally located, Father Branch moved the plant and offices to Moose Jaw in 1950. Management became a full time task for him. A total of 17 papers were being issued but finally the red ink of the ledgers overpowered the black and he was forced to abandon the business in 1952.

Mr. Ralph Purdy then appeared on the scene with considerable cash and he re-equipped the plant with more modern machinery and carried on the publication of most of the papers that Father Branch had issued.

But once again expenditures exceeded revenues and late in 1954 Mr. Purdy was visited by the sheriff with padlock and bailiff. Purdy hustled around, found a $50,000 angel and was allowed to carry on.

But the next year the sheriff again appeared and Mr. Gordon Hume, who desired to salvage some of the money he had previously invested in the operation, took it over and renamed the company Grand Valley Press Company.

He discontinued nine of the weeklies and set up a commercial printing department, but it was not until 1959 when he engaged a new manager that the business showed a profit.

In 1961, James R. Lovis purchased the business and published 10 newspapers until May, 1968, when due to lack of national and local advertising and high labor and material costs, all were abandoned. Mr. Lovis now operates the business solely as a job printing plant.

The second largest string of out-of-town weeklies was that promoted by J. Robert Long, who during the years previous to 1910, issued 14 publications. His plant was located at Caron, Sask.

Following the depression years, S. M. Bonneau of *The Gravelbourg Star* began issuing a number of weeklies for different towns in southwest Saskatchewan. This finally became the third largest string to be issued from one office. Turning his newspaper interests over to his son Paul, the latter, in 1961, was issuing 13 chain weeklies.

Records show that over 125 weeklies of this type were issued over the years out of a total of more than 525 town and village newspapers that were started in Saskatchewan beginning with the famous first—*The Battleford Herald*—begun by P. G. Laurie in 1878.

With the continuing disappearance of small town businesses, only a few out-of-town weeklies are presently being issued.

Chapter 17

DEPRESSION YEARS

Much has been written about the depression years of the 1930s, during which the Canadian prairie west suffered from the backlash of world economic break-down and crop failure brought on by the destructive action of drought and grasshoppers.

So much has been written, in fact, that further comment more than a third of a century later might appear ill-timed.

Yet, a backward glance will reveal conditions prevailing at the time that set in motion political, economic and social trends bringing a new way of life to all Canadians, a revolution still in the throes of development, as it is likely to be for years to come.

The sudden appearance of such large numbers of poor and unemployed brought a new concept of national responsibility for the welfare of all citizens.

Direct relief in the form of food, clothing and housing for those without, or with only the barest of means, created the duty of local, provincial and federal governments to provide, as best they could, the necessities required to sustain human life. Only the most cold-hearted could protest against this benevolence, limited as it was by necessity.

Of necessity it was a ministration carried out by officialdom rather than by neighbors, for the simple reason the latter, as individuals, were all helpless financially to provide the material aid required, if indeed they were not on the border-line of poverty themselves.

When the real need had passed, the pattern had become set for further expansion into a great variety of government-sponsored plans providing various types of aid to individuals

112

and groups to an extent undreamed of half a century ago.

Springing from the fulfillment of a genuine need, the outcroppings now in evidence would appear unnecessary, had the same individual determination of the first Canadian pioneers not been weakened by the trying years of the 1930s.

Government paternalism is now well established in Canada for better or worse.

Yet the depression brought a full realization of true values of life to the generations living. The young of today have their own problems, as vital to them as the business of earning a living was to the youth of the 1930s. They have greater opportunities and greater training facilities and greater scope, hence their problems are greater.

The ever-present question, "what can I do, or, what should I do?" is the same as the youngsters of the depression years had, only in a different context.

For the years of the 1930s did away with some false standards, brought people to a fuller understanding of each other's problems, created closer friendships and proved that happiness and wholesome pleasures could be had at little monetary cost.

Yet, economic pressure changed the course and future of every type of commercial business and profession. Weekly newspapers were no exception.

The conditions which squeezed the smaller towns into villages, the villages into hamlets and the hamlets into road-side memories also restricted the incomes of all weekly newspapers.

While the greatest number of casualties among weekly newspapers did not take place during the 1930s but rather in the mid-forties, the financial resources of their owners became impaired or even wiped out through curtailed volume of business and reduced flow of cash.

There were a few publishers who found it necessary to accept some measure of government relief, while continuing to issue their newspapers at no profit, with confidence that good times would eventually return to put their business once more on sound financial footing.

Few of these, if any, survived to see their visions become a reality. Publication of their newspapers ceased.

Some owners were able to move their plants to more promising locations, mainly in the northern part of Saskatchewan. Others sought employment as printers or as writers with city dailies. In both fields they were mostly successful, if underpaid.

The number of newspapers discontinued would have been much smaller had the publishers been able to collect their subscription price in cash from every subscriber. This small amount, usually two dollars, or less, per year, never loomed so large and vitally important in keeping a business solvent as it did during those years of stress.

The cash which the newspaperman needed to pay for his newsprint was never fully available.

In the southwest corner of Saskatchewan, farm land suffered the most from gales which ripped the top soil from every field to create over most of the drought years the largest area of barren wheatland in the province.

A large portion of this section was served by *The Shaunavon Standard,* which continued mailing its issues weekly to every subscriber in arrears with an optimistic hope that each "next year" would bring spring rains, green fields and a rich golden harvest, making possible the payment of the debts.

Finally, *The Standard* could no longer stand the financial strain.

W. E. Sharp, then its publisher, recalls the situation:

"I simply could not continue to send my paper to those in arrears of subscription. One week I cut off 300 names from the mailing list. Each one owed me for five or six years."

Asked if he later collected much of these arrears, he said, "Yes, after another five or six years went by and conditions had improved, quite a number voluntarily paid what they owed me."

The story of how John A. Vopni of *The Davidson Leader* defied the economic pressures of the "dirty thirties," is almost unbelievable. During this period, his efforts carried him into the more prosperous years with a firmly established business, and a subscription list that had more than tripled.

John, the eldest of a family of six, had previously apprenticed himself to the printing trade with *"Loberg,"* an Icelandic weekly published in Winnipeg. He was incidentally, the means of starting four of his brothers in the printing trade.

He purchased *The Davidson Leader* in 1931, rather than face the uncertainties of employment in the city. The business was housed in a two-story building and five stoves were used to keep the office, work shop and upstairs apartment warm.

John soon realized that he had taken over a business at a time when subscriptions were falling into arrears and cash settlements were rare. Commercial printing was scarce, with most businessmen using plain writing paper and envelopes instead of printed stationery.

He began considering some way whereby he could get his subscribers to pay with produce that in turn could be turned into cash. He soon decided that poultry would be the medium of exchange as chickens were being raised on nearly every farm.

Day after day, he drove into the country calling at farm after farm, following daily planned routes, offering to take hens in payment of arrears of subscription, or for new ones. There were days he gathered up as many as 90 birds. Once he had 150 in his chicken house but it so happened that all of them flew out of a window that had been left open. It took a lot of time, trouble and ruffled temper to catch them, but in a sense, his time then was not too valuable.

He would make regular shipments to city buyers and in this manner received cash returns, far beyond what he might otherwise have collected. Certainly, the five stoves were kept well stocked with fuel during chilly weather.

The result was that the number of paid-in-advance subscribers to *The Leader* increased from the 300 he had acquired with the purchase of the business up to nearly 1000. This at a time when weekly subscription lists were dwindling at an alarming rate.

He realized, however, that new subscribers could not be retained unless news from their respective districts appeared regularly in his paper. So he increased the number of his country correspondents to 40, thus establishing a list of loyal subscribers throughout an unusually large area. Over the years, John Vopni's effort remains as an example of a fine accomplishment in the face of most adverse conditions.

But there were a few bright spots to ease the drudgery.

John tells of having one day sent his younger brother, William, out to the country because he was unable to go himself. It was a trip producing a story which became a headliner for community chit-chat for some time.

Will knew how to barter, all right, but at one place the farmer's wife was the only one at home. He had no trouble in making a deal with her for chickens but it was up to him to catch the birds and put them into the cage on his truck.

He had begun to gather them up, one at a time, when the farmer's wife rather firmly said: "I want you to take roosters, not hens."

This was a poser for Will. He had to have the difference between roosters and hens explained to him.

Before he had completed his day's route, the rural telephone lines were buzzing. When he got back to Davidson, that night, it seemed that everyone in town and country had heard the story. Needless to say he became the butt of a lot of hilarious comment about sending an ignorant city boy out to deal with farmers.

It was but natural that John Vopni occasionally picked up a few pounds of butter or some potatoes, rather than chickens, but he was just as likely to find someone willing to part with a partridge or a duck, a piece of fresh meat or a sack of wheat that could be ground into grits, all of which reduced materially the cash outlay for groceries.

Dr. Sam Wynn of *The Yorkton Enterprise* solved his subscription arrears problem in another way. He visited grain buyers, signed them up as subscription agents and agreed to accept wheat storage tickets in lieu of cash for his paper.

Wheat at that time was only worth around 30 cents per bushel, but Sam was prepared to accept three bushels as payment of the regular one dollar subscription price.

Eventually he had several thousand bushels in storage which he held until the price of wheat had advanced sufficiently to provide him with a profit.

S. M. Bonneau, owner of *The Gravelbourg Star* was also a practicing barrister.

He recalls that there was little or no cash income from his law practice in the depression years, but by travelling over his district and bartering for farm produce in payment of subscriptions he was able to keep his home larder amply stocked.

In later reminiscences, Arthur Menzies, publisher of *The Hudson Bay Junction Judge* from 1931 to 1936, tells of some of the rather unusual things that happened there:

"We arrived at the Junction late in 1931. We were among the millions who had suddenly found themselves bereft of the good incomes they had enjoyed during the Roaring Twenties and we moved to the Junction in the hope that it would afford an anchorage where we could ride out the economic storm.

"The depression continued until 1939, when the country went to war and under the magic auspices of wholesale waste and destruction, we were suddenly prosperous again.

"During the depression years, most of the people in the Junction, as elsewhere, lived hand to mouth. Only those with steady jobs knew for certain what would produce the next day's groceries. There was a surplus of every kind of goods but no money.

"One day a man came into our office and bought a copy of the paper for five cents. The next cash we took in was a week later when the same man came in for a paper."

The next portion of Mr. Menzies' story might well be heeded in the present lavish age by those with relatively high incomes who find it difficult to make ends meet.

He wrote: "How does one provide for a family under conditions like these? It sounds impossible, but somehow it was done. And in spite of the impossible conditions, we did not go into debt, and even bettered our capital condition substantially.

"We exchanged the paper for cordwood, meat, vegetables—any portable property of value. Even buttermilk. One day a man offered us a gallon of buttermilk a week for a whole year in exchange for a subscription to the paper.

We suggested that where there is so much buttermilk there must be some butter. How about a few pounds of butter? Not a chance, said the man—butter could be sold at the store.

"There was a wood deal between the Village and Canadian National Railway in which the former acted as intermediary between the homesteader supplying the wood and the company.

"When the homesteader delivered a load of wood to the railway roundhouse, the Village issued a piece of scrip reading as follows: 'The Village of Hudson Bay Junction acknowledges an indebtedness to the bearer of (25c, 50c, $1, $2, etc.). Present this to the Village secretary at the end of the month.'

"The first day the scrip hit the street, a chartered bank applied to the courts for permission to prosecute the Village for issuing money. But the courts would not permit an action to be launched because there was no promise to pay. When we left the Junction the scrip was still circulating."

Only those who lived during the depression years know what degree of effort had to be made to earn a dollar.

Newspapermen and printers were no exceptions to others in striving to keep their businesses operating, regardless of what it cost them in wear and tear on their equipment.

It could be said they were living on depreciation.

So long as newspapermen operated their plants, they could seek advertising and job printing. A defunct business with closed premises simply eliminated that possibility.

The result was that in bidding for business, most owners who were also printers, quoted prices that were quite ridiculous, in order to get jobs, so long as they wound up with a little cash money. It was cash receipts, not barter dollars, which enabled them to keep off relief rolls.

Walter Ashfield, of *The Grenfell Sun*, was one who very definitely displayed determination to battle for those cash dollars no matter at what physical cost in terms of hours worked.

Retail storekeepers carrying stocks of general merchandise were no exception to those needing cash. Many had large stocks that were not moving and which they were prepared to offer at cost or near cost in order to get cash with which to liquidate their wholesale accounts.

Here was a real situation for the right man to capitalize upon. There was one gentleman who made a specialty of promoting "Close Out," "Stock Reduction," "Thrilling Discount," "Gigantic Clearance," and other similarly titled sales, all of which were a startling innovation in rural merchandising.

This man was an expert at displaying goods, calculating discounts, crowding table and counter tops with piles of items creating an atmosphere that challenged people to buy. To start this off, the area for miles beyond the normal shopping territory, would be flooded with big posters that screamed with bargain prices.

Walter made a deal with this enterprising gentleman. Each would drive half way to a central point where copy, and layout for the posters would change hands.

Walter would then drive home, set the type for the poster, which was always 24x36 inches in size, print 1000 copies in most cases, fold them ready for mailing and drive back to the midway point to deliver them to the promoter, all within 24 hours.

Only those acquainted with the limitations of plant and staff in the average country printing office could realize what a feat this was.

For all the travel, and the work of producing the job, including cost of the paper stock, Walter received $25.

Previous to the depression of a normal price for this job, less travel, would have been upwards of three times that amount.

In my own business I had a heart-warming experience never to be forgotten because of its manifestation of the co-operation prevailing among people living at nearly the same economic level and filled with the spirit of sharing.

Enterprise Show Print business rose to its peak of volume during the spring and summer months. As this work required specially trained printers and pressmen, I found it best to keep these key men on the staff all the year around, rather than fire and rehire, or else train new men when the busy season opened.

When the pressure began towards the end of March, these poster men would work like slaves. They appreciated being kept on all winter at full pay in semi-idleness and tried in this manner to make repayment for the consideration. They would maintain the pace as long as the work was on hand.

During 1931, there came a marked falling-off in business volume, in both poster and newspaper business and it became quite apparent that I had too large a staff. But which of these loyal employees would I discharge? To lose one's job meant entry into the poverty stricken horde of unemployed.

Week after week, when payday came around, the old problem came with it. Each week the thought of laying off any of them became increasingly painful.

The final decision was made by the staff members themselves.

One Saturday morning, they all came into my office with the foreman as spokesman. They had talked the situation over. It was quite apparent to them that the amount of business being done could not support the prevailing payroll.

They had a proposition to make.

They would all take a ten per cent cut in the hourly rate then being paid them and work only the number of hours needed to produce our work providing such did not go below 30 hours per week.

Their offer brought tears to my eyes. They had solved the problem themselves, in a much fairer manner than I could have done. As time went on, one man had friends pick up a job for him at the coast, then another found employment elsewhere, and soon the staff was of proper size and the rate of pay back to the former level.

All this was an action on the part of labor that stood out as an excellent example of good judgement on the part of a staff who would not demand the impossible of an employer suffering a business setback.

However, the background of those days were different. Industrial staffs were in most cases quite small when compared with those of modern times, and non-unionized. Personal

daily contact between employer and worker developed friend-
ship and understanding of each others' problems and needs
and anxieties. It was a far cry from the type of "arms length"
relationships which exist today between labor and management. Perhaps this is just one of the penalties of technological
progress, but one can become nostalgic about the benefits
of the friendly atmosphere of an earlier day.

It was in the mid-depression years that I participated
in an experience which revealed how innocently and unwittingly one can become involved in a shady operation.
Yet I cannot help but think that many printers were not too
concerned about enquiring into the status of new customers
during those trying days. More business was the one thing
everyone desired most.

A man who ran a small typewriter repair shop in Regina,
and whom I knew only casually, came into my office one
day accompanied by an elderly gentleman, refined in manner
and speech, impeccably dressed, and with the personality
of a successful businessman.

After being introduced, the stranger explained that he
was representing a mutual benefit association which was
operating in Manitoba. They were considering extending
their operations into Saskatchewan. He wanted prices on
tickets and receipt forms which they might need.

Previous to that time, several such associations had been
operating throughout the west in a manner which gave them
a reputable standing. They paid out sick benefits to ailing
ticket holders in accord with their avowed objectives—a
mutual benefit association. I had known a friend in Rouleau
who had received $200 following a surgical operation from one
in which he held membership. This particular organization
had been started and carried on by a group of railwaymen
for their own benefit.

After giving the visitor all the information he desired as
to price and so on, he said that if his organization decided on
moving into Saskatchewan, orders with payment accompanying, would come to me by mail.

Surprisingly, the first order came two days later. It was

rather a small one, but any size of order with cash on the barrelhead was eagerly welcomed.

A month later, a larger order came. Then with each succeeding month the orders became larger until the accompanying cash payments reached quite a substantial figure. They became highlights in the dismal financial picture of depression times.

The printing was shipped by express to Regina to the man who ordered it, care of the typewriter shop. Wishing to meet the buyer in person, I took an opportunity when in that city to look him up. The people at the typewriter shop told me he only used its address for delivery of mail and express. They had no idea where he lived.

I thought this a bit queer, but realized that city ways were not the familiar small town ways.

One day, after I had completed and packed for shipment, the largest order ever, the man called me from Regina telling me just to hold it until he advised me later. He explained that a complaint of some kind had been lodged against his organization but he was confident an explanation to the authorities would straighten everything out.

But his last words were alarming when he said: "Just in case, destroy all records of transactions with me." Such action was out of the question, for they were sprinkled all through our ledgers and bank deposit slips.

I didn't sleep too well that night.

The next morning he 'phoned to say that everything had been cleared up and he would be over to pick up the printing the next evening, which he did.

I asked him about his trouble, and how he managed to get it ironed out so quickly. He quietly said: "It always pays to have something on someone higher up!"

The reality of the whole situation suddenly exploded in my mind. I was startled to realize that my good customer was part of a gangster group that was smoothly duping and robbing the public.

I immediately told him that I would do no more printing for him. He tried to persuade me to change my mind, finally saying: "You know we never tell anyone where we get our printing done, but if by chance the secret gets out and you should be in trouble we will always protect you!"

There was only one kind of reply to give him. It was "I don't want your protection. I'll protect myself. You're no longer a customer of mine."

I had only been a single step away from being enmeshed with the underworld.

A short time later, all traces of the organization vanished. Someone higher up in the legal structure who could not be intimidated had quite evidently taken fast and effective action.

William Charles Needham of *The Wynyard Advance* was one of the few weekly newspapermen who emerged from the depression years with a much increased subscription list.

After he had taken over the business in 1938 and moved his family to Wynyard, he found himself with exactly $2.50 in cash in his trousers pocket. This situation stirred him to consider some fast money-raising action.

He instituted a subscription contest with a new automobile as first prize. This was probably the first time in Saskatchewan weekly newspaper history that such a prize was offered. When the contest started, his subscription list was approximately 300. When it closed it was four times that number or very close to 1300.

Contestants collected $1.50 for a year's subscription. The winner of the car was the one contestant who never refused to accept farm produce in payment, and gathered hundreds of chickens for which there was a cash market. He no doubt added to the amount of his small commission by whatever profit he might make between the amount he allowed the subscriber for the poultry and what he received in cash from the wholesale dealer.

After the contest closed, Mr. Needham counted his surplus takings. They amounted to $250—a munificent sum in those days.

Chapter 18

SPECIAL TALENTS

Throughout the years many publishers of weekly newspapers exhibited special talents in differing phases of
their operations. While such attributes did not exactly
attract nation-wide attention, they gave those who displayed
them a degree of distinction throughout the printing fraternity.

In some cases, the mechanical phase provided them with
the greatest satisfaction. These were the ones who took pride
in keeping their machinery in tip-top shape and maybe by
the addition of some little gadget of their own invention,
improved the productivity of one of their machines.

Others concentrated on their writing, whether it was news
reporting, editorial writing, or maybe free-lance writing for
faraway publications of which local readers were not aware.

Others made a fetish of typographical excellence and the
production of the best possible printing their plant could
produce, the while always searching for or originating new
ideas in printing technique.

Within the latter group comes W. D. Morphy, publisher
of *The Biggar Independent*, who took on the challenge of the
Saskatchewan Farmers Union and the Royal Canadian
Mounted Police to develop a fool proof method of "Branding"
grain stored in farmer's granaries and bins.

The idea was to produce a "confetti" of little squares of
paper, each printed with tiny figures.

Initially, it seemed a simple matter of just printing sheets
of paper and cutting them up in the size required, but Morphy
knew it was not that elementary, even though printing of
tiny numbers properly positioned on a fair-sized piece of paper
was only a routine bit of typesetting and presswork.

But how to cut the paper, after printing, into pieces one-half inch by one-quarter inch in size, with a few numbers on every piece was a puzzle to challenge any inventive mind.

There never was a paper cutting machine manufactured to cut pieces of paper that size with the accuracy demanded. Then with a pound of the confetti requiring about 100,000 of the little pieces, the cost of cutting had to be kept at a very low figure.

For days and nights Mr. and Mrs. Morphy's conscious and subconscious minds did little else than try to solve the problem. Often one of them would wake up in the early morning hours with a new idea as to how the job could be done, only to toss it aside after analyzing it later, during more wide-awake hours.

Finally they came up with a practical method known only to themselves. No one can blame them for keeping it a deep secret.

Mr. Morphy sells the finished confetti in five pound lots containing about 500,000 pieces, each carrying the number allotted to a farmer when he buys a supply. This number is registered and kept on file for the RCMP.

Farmers mix these bits of paper with their grain as they pour the latter into their bins. The pieces cannot all be removed except by elaborate machinery usually found only in flour mills.

Morphy also keeps a sample of paper and ink used on each different batch of numbers for possible laboratory tests.

The RCMP report that many granaries are broken into, but thefts of grain rarely follow from bins in which this confetti has been sprinkled. The main value of the "branding" technique is its obvious deterrent effect on theft.

It seems that most thefts still committed are made by marginal farmers who use the stolen grain as feed for their animals which eat the incriminating evidence along with the grain.

Certainly if branded grain were taken to an elevator by someone unknown to the agent the latter would simply record the number on the confetti, and check with the RCMP or Morphy to quickly ascertain whether or not the vendor was the rightful owner.

O. D. Stitt, *Radville Star*; R. S. Reid, *Kindersley Clarion*; John A. Vopni, *Davidson Leader* and George Baynton, *Lloydminster Times*, were gifted in a somewhat unusual way.

All were linotype operators, like nearly all weekly newspaper publishers. But unlike others they did not need to write or typewrite "copy" of news stories such as linotype operators of the rank and file require to follow as they operate the machine in the routine commonly referred to as "setting the type."

These men would simply sit down at the linotype keyboard with their fingers touching the correct keys as their minds dictated the wording of the news to appear in the columns of the next issue.

This indicated that each had an unusual facility in putting news stories together without having to backtrack and revise sentences already set in type.

All of them had found that nothing was to be gained in first preparing the copy on a typewriter. By eliminating that task, time could be saved by just rattling the stuff off on the linotype keyboard and producing the slugs ready to fit into the columns of the newspaper forms.

It would likely be agreed that Bob Reid made greater use of this talent than others, in that he would also set up his editorials in the same manner. This probably required more premeditation on his part to arrange his thoughts in proper sequence, leading up to his final conclusions.

All of which is somewhat unusual as the average editorial writer's first draft is usually given a final polishing up before being turned over to the typesetter. Mr. Reid's editorials were always well constructed and rounded off. His writing ability in this field was recognized later when he was engaged as editor of the "Union Farmer."

On one occasion John Vopni had T. Melville-Ness, editor of The Western Producer, dictate a story of several columns in length dealing with the opening of a new Wheat Pool elevator in Davidson, while he just followed along, fingering out the words on the keyboard of his linotype.

John also tells a story of rare interest. While setting up his personal items such as "Mr. and Mrs. Smith left on Tuesday for . . ." he found that trouble had developed in the channel of the linotype magazine carrying the periods.

Under deadline pressure, he by-passed immediate correction of the mechanical trouble by omitting the period after all the Mr. and Mrs.

He expected to hear comment about such omissions but was more than surprised that not one reader, at any time, ever mentioned it. So it became a style which he carried on in his news columns.

His experience recalls a previous "period-removing" sweep over the North American continent, breaking down an international custom that had prevailed over the centuries since the beginning of printing.

One would hardly think that a dot, the smallest possible mark made by pen or type, could have been the cause of such a fuss.

Books, of course, were the first product of the printing press. The title of a book was considered a sentence. Therefore a period was placed at the end of every book title, even though it was only a single word. A check on all ancient volumes in museums and private libraries will provide proof of this.

This custom was continued with the coming of tracts, bulletins of all sorts, and newspapers, when every heading ended with a period. The style was carried into advertising, no matter in what form, when such began to appear in newspapers.

The first Canadian newspapers quite naturally carried on the custom. Suddenly at the turn of the century leading American printing houses and newspapers decided that periods so placed were unnecessary, and proceeded to omit them.

This decision was a disturbing one to Canadian printers and publishers who, quite naturally, had sentimental ties with overseas practices and routines, particularly with those used in Britain.

The absence of the little black dots at the end of a heading or subheading in American newspapers and other printed matter was almost shocking. It seemed as though printers had become careless in a product requiring the highest degree of accuracy.

I can remember quite well when Canadian printers began to accept the innovation, but for a time, from force of habit, they would unthinkingly drop in the period at a headline's end. Eventually all printers got accustomed to the practice.

But typographical arrangements are constantly changing, particularly in advertising. To avoid monotony, new type styles and type arrangements are designed.

Maybe it is not at all strange that in the search for diversions to catch the eye, many national advertisers have recently resurrected the old use of the period by placing it at the end of the main heading of their newspaper or magazine advertisements.

No one will deny that this use of the little black dot adds power and punch to such lines with their impressionable usage of words.

But whoever thought that the period would again be used in the ancient manner after years of oblivion?

Subscribers of weekly newspapers are not always fully aware of the literary capacity of their editors. Local readers rate editors in the manner in which local affairs are reported with little thought of the possibility that news writing may not bring out an editor's real capabilities.

Some Saskatchewan editors have achieved remarkable success in faraway places about which the home-town folk have little, if any, knowledge.

One most outstanding in this regard is William David Belbeck, who joined the staff of *The Swift Current Sun* in 1944 as reporter, and in 1957, became its editor and part owner.

After leaving school in 1921, he longed to get into the newspaper business but the closest he could come was a job as advertising manager for a departmental store in Swift Current and later in the same capacity for one at Weyburn.

He returned to Swift Current in 1930, and for the next few years supported himself and family by freelance writing.

He had sold his first story to *Argosy* magazine when he was 18 years old, but his biggest thrill must have come when *The Saturday Evening Post* accepted the very first story he sent to it.

For years, scores of writers hoped and prayed that their

literary efforts might appear in that magazine. In those days it was the aristocrat among magazines with the largest circulation by far of all American magazines, being the first to acquire more than one million subscribers.

The *Post* was most fastidious in its selection of stories and articles, but paid all contributors most generously. To be accepted into this rare coterie was a reward in itself.

Magazines which carried Belbeck's writings were *Collier's, Chatelaine, Star Weekly, Country Guide,* the English *20-story Magazine, Western Home Monthly,* as well as many others.

He contributed a great deal to United Church publications. Dave himself has said that he did so much writing for these that eventually his pay cheques came addressed to "Rev. Dave Belbeck."

There was Peter D. Dales, who for four years wrote a family serial for CBC radio while moving about doing relief agent's work for the C.P.R. It was a story of a western farm family, titled "Youngbloods of Beaver Bend" and was heard weekly from coast to coast. To produce a half hour story every week is a task that calls for a writer of special aptitude.

The style of writing for stage or screen is not at all the same as for news reporting when the stories are already realities which only need to be reduced to essential facts.

A fiction story requires a mind that can vividly project various vagaries of human character into contacts and situations expressing explicitly a definite play of human emotions.

Anyone who could, for a succession of years, compose a weekly installment of a story fascinating enough to induce people by the thousands to turn on their radios at a specified hour can be rated as a writer of singular talent.

While Mr. Dales was not at that time associated with the weekly newspaper business, he began publication of *The Mainliner* while railway agent at Ernfold in 1951, becoming a full-fledged newspaperman on purchasing *The Herald* at Herbert.

Of all editorial writers and reporters affiliated with Saskatchewan weeklies, Ken Mayhew was recognized as the most fluent, productive and versatile.

Ken came from Renfrew, Ontario, in 1928 to become a

reporter for *The Yorkton Enterprise*. In sequence, he became its news editor, assistant manager, associate editor and finally editor under the tutelage of Dr. S. N. Wynn. His death occurred in 1960.

The speed with which he could turn out copy was fantastic. His fingers on the typewriter keyboard never had to wait an instant for the words and sentences his clear-thinking mind assembled. He had the ability to arrange his material facts in proper sequence so rapidly as to enable him to dash off news stories without any backtracking or confusing paragraphs.

In reporting one election eve political meeting at which a cabinet minister announced government policy, Ken, within a few hours, filed eight columns of copy so accurate in its context that it was reprinted without correction to become one of the party's most informative campaign publications.

His colorful reports on a score of murder trials, the Kamsack cyclone and sports features appeared in most Canadian dailies, Maclean's Magazine, Liberty, Time, Newsweek and sports magazines.

It was in this type of writing that he excelled, even though he won distinction as a top editorial writer winning many awards for *The Yorkton Enterprise*, not only because of his grasp of federal, provincial and municipal politics, but because of the practical manner in which he discussed topics involving commonly-held opinions of great variance.

He had a burning zeal for the promotion of brotherhood among nations and religious groups, and this theme not only characterised much of his writing and speaking, but won for him a legion of friends across Canada and the United States.

His weekly column "Kenny Says" was his literary show window, and through the years displayed his knowledge of many subjects with his humanism ever enriching discussion of current topics.

Though he was full of energy, one could only wonder how he found time for all his activities. For years he was associated with provincial and amateur hockey associations, editor of *Saskatchewan Hockey Annual* for 25 years, a loyal service club member, assisted innumerable welfare societies and drives, and was in demand as a public speaker throughout Canada and the United States, where on one occasion he was honored with an appointment as honorary Lieutenant-Colonel on the staff of the governor of Texas.

The majority of weekly newspapermen in western Canada began their careers in youth as apprentices in the printing trade in which they in due course became proficient.

Of necessity, during this training period, they became familiar with platen and cylinder presses. While these were very simply constructed as compared with those of later years, the embryo printers had at times to face situations for which they were ill prepared. Very few of them had previously any contact with machines of any kind. The full impact of the machine age had not touched the nation's frontiers.

When something went amiss with a press, they had to deduce the cause of the trouble and how it could be overcome. In this manner, they learned a great deal of elementary mechanics. It was all simply a case of must. The nearest other printer who might be able to give advice and help was most likely miles away, and there were no telephones.

However, this scant education and the manner in which it had been obtained prepared most of them for the coming of the linotype and new types of presses, automatic and otherwise, with all their intricate parts. They were high-precision machines, requiring careful adjustment and operation to produce a better product with greater speed and efficiency.

The physical science of mechanics had become a permanent partner with the art of printing.

Many of these self-trained printers in country shops moved into cities to accept top positions involving the care or use of machines.

But there were still others, mainly owners of newspapers, remaining in country offices who advanced into the field of invention to a degree that surprised even the makers of printing machinery.

One of these was Fred Batty, publisher of *The Independent* at Wawanesa, Manitoba. He had purchased one of the first automatic job presses offered to printers. It was an excellent machine, very much advanced over all others at the time.

Batty overlooked asking one question before buying and installing it and that question was "will it print envelopes?" He found out quickly enough that it was not designed to do that type of work. He had one customer who used hundreds of thousands of envelopes each year, so the inability of the press to print them was a major disappointment.

After operating it for a few days on flat paper jobs and becoming familiar with the operation of the machine, he invented a little gadget, constructed it so that it could be attached to the press when an order of envelopes was to be printed and forever afterwards the envelopes whizzed through the press at its top speed.

He had out-paced the high-priced, highly trained inventive geniuses at the factory.

George Baynton who bought *The Times* at Lloydminster, Saskatchewan in 1940, had an academic background. He was then not a printer but he quickly developed a familiarity with the printing trade and its machines.

He maintained a forward look at all times, keeping an eye and ear keenly in tune with mechanical improvements, something that had not been necessary in his previous profession.

His newspaper was first printed on a cylinder press, four pages at a time. Circulation growth and increased number of pages with every issue made it quite evident a machine with greater capacity was needed.

There were satisfactory flat-bed rotary presses manufactured at that time, using newsprint from a roll and turning out complete eight page sections with one run, and at three times the speed of a sheet fed cylinder press. The cost of installing a new one involved a substantial number of dollars.

Mr. Baynton found himself between two pressures. He needed a press of that type, but his business, while on the upturn, could barely afford the cost of a new machine.

He learned of one that had been used but rated to be in poor condition. Occasionally there are precision machines of all kinds turned out that have some mechanical imperfection. This one could be purchased for a very small sum.

He bought it, moved it to his plant, and began to put

it together in his spare time, a job that normally would be done by a factory-trained erector.

Parts were checked for wear and new replacements bought. Finally it was complete and ready to run. And run it did—perfectly.

This was not the end of the happy story. Baynton, while putting the machine together had developed ideas as to how it might be made to operate more efficiently. So he made a few attachments which enabled the machine to turn out work it had been unable to do before.

It requires no stretch of the imagination to sense that country printers in the early years were frequently faced with breakage of a machine part at some critical time, maybe press day. Usually the nearest source of new parts was either Toronto or Vancouver. If old type machines were involved, factory-made parts were no longer available.

Replacements in such cases usually required whatever ingenuity the local machinist or the printer himself could muster. Rarely did either or both fail to come through, like Bob Reid of *The Kindersley Clarion* who in 1946 fashioned an immediately-needed repair for his linotype out of a piece of copper. It turned out to be a permanent part. Sixteen years later it was still functioning satisfactorily.

A survey of western country printers would most likely show that the type of ingenuity demonstrated by Bob Reid and others, was not at all unusual.

Chapter 19

NEWSPAPER INFLUENCE

During the summer, and until the first snows of winter have fallen, the alternate strips of crop and black fallow land covering the rolling hills and lesser slopes of prairie fields in the Shaunavon district in south-western Saskatchewan, present a tapestry of unusual beauty.

The undulations of the hills whose tops break the pattern only to have it renewed in lesser dimension on the more distant headlands, serve to intensify its eye appeal, which is still more accentuated as seasons bring change of coloring from the lush green of spring to the autumn gold of ripening grain.

One need not have an acute artistic sense to heed the picturesque scene when driving through the heart of this regenerated farm land area during any season of the year.

Yet this bit of outdoor beauty was not developed in response to a cultural urge. It was brought about through rehabilitation of a countryside tottering on the brink of financial ruin.

Known as "strip farming"—a method of erosion control—it brought thousands of acres of seriously damaged land back into profitable production of grain.

Of immediate interest is the knowledge that the first impetus was given the initiation of strip farming in this area through the planning, urging and pleading of *The Shaunavon Standard* early in the drought-stricken years of the 1930s.

The project was an outstanding example of what a live weekly newspaper can do in providing initiative and leadership in promoting sound projects for community advancement.

134

In the earlier years of farming in Western Canada, topsoil drifting caused by strong winds and drought had not been a serious matter. But lack of moisture in any form and winds of high velocity prevailed during the 1930s. The valuable top-soil, for several inches deep, was whipped from the fields and driven across their surface with a force that no vegetation could resist.

While the routine of strip farming originated at the Dominion Experimental Farm at Lethbridge, Alberta, and used in certain small areas in that district, it had not been practiced to any extent elsewhere in Western Canada.

It could only achieve complete success where every farmer in a relatively large block of land participated. Farm-ers were hesitant to adopt the practice because of the initial upset in their normal crop planting routine, and switching to a two-year, rather than a three-year rotation.

W. E. Sharp and R. L. Sanborn, owners of *The Shaunavon Standard*, were well aware that the only hope of halting wind erosion of the sparse topsoil was through the practice of strip farming.

They climaxed a convincing editorial campaign of some week's duration by organizing a mass meeting of farmers, to hear Bill Reid, a man who had been successful in persuading Montana farmers to adopt the strip farming technique.

"Summerfallow Bill" presented his story with such ardor that an association was immediately formed and eventu-ally every farmer in the Shaunavon district joined in the movement.

The original promotion so ably charted by Sharp and Sanborn eventually reached far beyond their original concept. It was only a few years until strip farming, with its many practical advantages, extended far beyond the immediate Shaunavon area.

The influence of the weekly newspaper in shaping eco-nomic and social trends within the community it serves may not always be as spectacular or as far-reaching as the Shauna-von experience.

In many instances a local interest in some worthwhile community activity has been gradually built up and established by unassuming leadership by the local newspaperman through expression of editorial opinion or in the more intimate comment of the casual column now carried by many weeklies.

There is little doubt but that newspapers with good standards of news coverage, editorial comment and business management, commanding respect of their readers, can influence the initiation of a local trend or movement and keep it moving and active so long as a need for it exists.

An example of this is to be found in Gull Lake, Saskatchewan. It all began back in the days of the late Harold Gamble who, through his weekly newspaper, *The Advance*, stressed and promoted recreation in different forms.

His policy has been continued by his son, Ford, and his wife, Anne, who, recognizing the importance of projects most helpful to young people, have channeled their support and interest mainly in that direction.

Their influence begins right in their own office. The *Advance* carries a column, " 'Teen-Temple," edited by boys and girls, whose comments are certainly far from immature.

The emphasis on youth activities embraces most of the organizations in the town, which in similar number could hardly be expected to be found in other than a small city at least.

There is a music association which for 20 years has been putting on Sunday evening musicales, encouraging budding talent to perform in public; a recreation board which sponsors art competitions and financially assists other community projects such as musical productions and a week of fine arts; a high school drama club; a school band of over 100 members; a riding and roping club; 4-H clubs; CGIT; Girl Guides and Boy Scouts; an association sponsoring senior and minor sports; a high school football team that was twice provincial champion; a Chamber of Commerce primarily interested in hockey and football teams; a curling and skating rink; and numerous others.

Mr. and Mrs. Gamble, through the columns of their newspaper, continue to inspire the continuation of these wholesome community activities and locally, *The Advance* is recognized as a most effective influence in maintaining the high cultural level of which the town of Gull Lake is so proud.

While the two examples quoted are outstanding, it is more difficult to recognize the everyday type of community activity which is stimulated to a marked degree by a short series of publicity items in the columns of the weekly newspapers.

Every one of these in Saskatchewan, from time to time as the occasion may have warranted, has participated in such promotion. A typical example is that of Bob Reid of *The Kindersley Clarion*, and his campaign to promote interest in clinics of the Red Cross Blood Donor service through editorials and news items. This resulted over the years in Kindersley collecting far more blood than other centers with five to six times the population.

With the number of weekly newspapers on the prairies gradually dwindling, rural communities affected are losing more than simply one business establishment. They will suffer more from the departure of that force which has unostentatiously stimulated local activities and progress—the creative influence of a respected weekly newspaper.

Chapter 20

THE FAMOUS FOUR SAMS

The "Famous Four Sams" from the ranks of Saskatchewan weekly newspapermen had more than a common Christian name to link them together.

They shared also dedication to a cause—that of promoting the welfare of all members of Saskatchewan Division, Saskatchewan Weekly Newspapers Association.

These four men were: Sam Moore of *The Swift Current Sun,* Sam Dornan of *The Alameda Dispatch,* Sam Latta of *The Govan Prairie News* and Sam Wynn of *The Yorkton Enterprise.*

During the 1920s, their combined efforts were mainly responsible for establishing within the CWNA Saskatchewan Division a calibre of newspaper standards not excelled by any other provincial group in Canada.

They not only urged a higher level of journalistic proficiency and ethics, typographical excellence and better business methods: they themselves upheld these standards in the operation of their own newspapers.

It was mainly through their influence that Saskatchewan weeklies began to multiply their winnings of awards in the various classes of annual national competitions. It was an influence so deeply rooted that many Saskatchewan weeklies have continued to win top honors in Canadian Weekly Newspapers Associations contests.

It was early in the most active years of the Famous Four Sams that every eligible weekly newspaper in the province was a member of the Saskatchewan Division, a record not duplicated by any other provincial association in Canada.

Each of the Four Sams had different talents and distinctive personalities. This had much to do with the cumulative success they achieved through their promotional efforts.

Sam Moore had the politician's discernment of human nature. He had oratorical powers which earned him a rating of one of the most talented speakers among all parliamentarians in Canada. He knew when and how to stir the feelings of an audience with convincing words and melodious phrases. In this regard he excelled when addressing public groups with which newspapers had reason to maintain contacts.

Sam Dornan was outspoken, quick to air his knowledge and beliefs, yet considerate in listening to the ideas of others. His judgement was respected by all who knew of his close contact with and knowledge of the newspaper business. There were few in Canada who were as well versed in technicalities of national advertising. He could bring an entire convention to attention when, in his Irish brogue, he would begin, "Mister-r-r Chair-r-r-man. . ."

Sam Latta fitted into a unique role. He was a member of the Saskatchewan Legislative Assembly for 17 years, during 12 of which he held cabinet positions. Thus he was an inside advisor on association relationships with the government and vice versa, at times when each needed a better understanding on matters of dual interest.

Sam Wynn had a quiet, impressive dignity coupled with a keen business insight. When he discussed a subject his thoughts and beliefs were calmly expressed. Yet the rapidity with which he could voice the correct solution to a problem or unusual situation was most noteworthy.

Actually, each was a specialist in one of four distinct areas. The special talents and abilities of each complemented those of the others.

One day Hon. Samuel J. Latta, then minister of education for Saskatchewan was told that the legislative committee of the Saskatchewan Press Association would like to consult him before attending a special meeting with the premier and cabinet.

"Tell them to come right in," said the genial minister, and in filed three other Samuels.

"Hello, Sam," said Samuel R. Moore.

"Hello, Sam," said Samuel J. Dornan.

"Hello, Sam," said Samuel N. Wynn.
"Hello, Sam, Sam, Sam," said the Hon. S. J. Latta.
Then they all laughed.

SAMUEL ROBERT MOORE

Born at Carbonear, Newfoundland, Mr. Moore came to Western Canada at the turn of the century. He began newspaper work at Fort William, Ontario, then in succession at Manitou, Manitoba; Moosomin and Regina Saskatchewan. In the latter city he was a reporter on *The West*, a weekly newspaper.

He went to Swift Current in 1908 as editor and manager of *The Sun* which had been moved there from Maple Creek in 1904 and had had something of an uncertain existence, due to changes of ownership and editors, and other publishing hazards of those early days.

From the very start in Swift Current he fitted in with the western atmosphere. In the Swift Current area there were some of the largest cattle ranges on the prairies.

He made his colorful personality felt in district and local affairs through his strong views on current topics, his love of life and people, and his booming laugh.

He was an orator of great ability, a courageous man, and one with the vision to foresee the development which was to come to the prairie west.

On the platform and from his editorial desk, he fought for policies that would be beneficial to a rapidly developing country.

When Walter Scott was premier of Saskatchewan Mr. Moore was elected Liberal member for the Pinto Creek constituency. He loved the game of politics and entered into it with gusto. With his newspaper and his voice he took part in those fiery, hectic political campaigns common to the first two decades after the turn of the century.

It was during the time Mr. Moore was a member of the Saskatchewan Legislative Assembly that some leading breweries incorporated hotel companies to secure for themselves greater control of the retailing of their particular brands of beer. One of these companies attempted to blanket the towns on the Weyburn-Shaunavon railway line.

A story—proof of which was never produced—told of how a new hotel was built in one of the towns by an independent operator and it of course had to be inspected under provincial health and sanitary regulations before a beer license could be issued to its owner. The story went on to relate that when an inspection was made, the building was found to be infested with bedbugs.

Because the town happened to be within Mr. Moore's constituency the story provided Bob Edwards' *Calgary Eye-Opener*, (ever eager to sensationalize its columns) with an opportunity to display on its front page a cartoon of a hotel bedroom with the bedclothes pulled back on the bed, and bedbugs running all over it.

This gave rise to the nickname "Bedbug Sam", used by Mr. Moore's friends; it did not remain in use for long.

Mr. Moore's interest in agriculture is well recorded in his support of the Saskatchewan Wheat Pool in its formative years.

He served as president of the Saskatchewan Division, Canadian Weekly Newspapers Association and as an active member of its parent body.

An accomplished raconteur with melodious voice he could deliver a speech on a moment's notice on an extensive range of subjects in a manner that always held an audience.

He retired from active newspaper work in February, 1933, when he sold his interest in *The Sun* to his son Robert, Mahlon Hutchison and Jim Greenblat, the latter becoming editor.

Mr. Moore died in 1949, at Nelson, B.C.

SAMUEL J. DORNAN

Coming from the Emerald Isle, Mr. Dornan had all the refreshing aplomb of the native Irishman, with a smile, a twinkle in his eye and an appreciation of the droll type of humor so characteristic of his race.

Behind this was a dynamic personality which only re-quired the thrill of a rapidly expanding prairie economy—

completely new to all immigrants from the old lands—to develop it into his chief asset in the business field.

It was shortly after he came to Canada that he purchased *The Alameda Dispatch* and settled down to a close study of the operation of his own small weekly newspaper, as well as others throughout the province, with the objective of making them more essential to their respective communities, and in turn receiving increased financial support.

Mr. Dornan was secretary-manager of the Saskatchewan Division, Canadian Weekly Newspapers Association from 1923 to 1947. He spearheaded the action to enroll every eligible weekly newspaper in the province as a member of the Association.

Then the securing of certain types of provincial advertising as well as national advertising for weekly newspapers became his next objective.

There were few executive advertising men either in advertising agencies or the offices of large manufacturing companies in Eastern Canada who, as a result of Mr. Dornan's persuasiveness, were not familiar with the superior coverage of rural population by the weekly press.

Conversely, he was able to advise weekly publishers how best they could conform to fixed requirements and blanket policies of those placing advertising for national campaigns of all descriptions.

In this regard, there was need to educate publishers of weekly newspapers to the fact that all too many of them were careless and sloppy in carrying on their business office routines.

Mr. Dornan kept reiterating the necessity of good bookkeeping practice, prompt mailing to agencies of voucher copies of their newspapers containing advertisements ordered, prompt billing and the use of standardized rate cards. In this regard he raised the standards of business methods of Saskatchewan weekly newspapermen to a comparatively high level.

He was a continuing source of information on various aspects of weekly newspaper work and during discussions at conventions was able to give helpful advice on every topic that arose.

His activities within the Saskatchewan Division were

mainly instrumental in bringing about the decision made by the Canadian Weekly Newspapers Association to employ a highly paid contact man in public relations work and promotion of national advertising in weekly newspapers throughout Canada.

When circumstances warranted, he would descend on heads of government at Ottawa to insure that weekly newspapers were not overlooked in the placing of advertising for special campaigns such as the sale of Victory Bonds during the Second World War. Neither did he hesitate to approach the proper cabinet members of his own provincial government to voice the need of timely advertising.

It was amazing how Mr. Dornan found time enough to serve so efficiently as manager of the Saskatchewan Division, CWNA, turn out his own weekly newspaper, (which was a consistent prize-winner), take an active part in civic and community affairs through serving on both Alameda town council and school board.

He was president of the Canadian Weekly Newspapers Association in 1931-32 and president of the Saskatchewan Division, 1947-48.

He was honored by the University of Saskatchewan with the degree of LL.D. and received in 1949 the first honorary life membership awarded by the Saskatchewan Division, CWNA.

He died March, 1959 at Alameda, Saskatchewan.

SAMUEL JOHN LATTA

As the first Minister of Highways for the Province of Saskatchewan, Samuel John Latta occupies a position of distinction in the history of Saskatchewan.

It was a cabinet appointment which first heralded the multitude of government responsibilities undreamed of in the early years of the century. It was the beginning of the new age when public administration began to change from a comparatively simple task to one of many complexities. It became necessary for governments to set up many new departments to keep in step with the demands of social, economic and scientific progress within the province.

143

The compulsion behind the setting up of the Department of Highways was the sharp increase in the number of automobile and truck owners, all clamoring for better roads and bridges.

The time had come when the haphazard network of prairie trails and municipal roads was outdated and it was only through the financial resources of the province they could be replaced by improved and extended roads to meet rapidly changing traffic requirements.

The day of the team and wagon, the horse and buggy was coming to an end. Even the graded, narrow dirt roads constructed by rural municipalities previously spotted here and there for short distances and looked upon as a vast improvement over rutted prairie trails, was failing to provide suitable service to the new form of speedier travel.

It was a stern challenge to Mr. Latta to be suddenly burdened with this unprecedented task with all its new problems. The construction of main arteries of traffic to meet the new and growing requirements was still in the experimental stage almost everywhere on the North American continent.

It called for the study of existing types of road building machinery, possible volume of traffic, road dimensions, soil conditions, along with the vexing problem of routing. There was only a scant amount of past experience to be found anywhere, providing a background on which to base new concepts that might properly serve future traffic needs.

The coming of motor vehicles had been swift and challenging. Their ultimate effect on future conditions was uncertain because mechanical limitations of earlier models and their ultimate degree of usefulness (or lack of it) were factors that had to be taken into account.

Yet Mr. Latta established a highway program stretching into the future, involving varied types of construction and proposed routings that needed few corrections during the passing of years.

To those lacking an intimate knowledge of Mr. Latta's talents his success in administering the new department of highways might come as a surprise, but he had already proven himself to be one who could adjust quickly to new responsibilities.

At the beginning of his public career he was known as an educationist who enjoyed teaching, and later as an artist, author, farmer, newspaperman and politician.

Born at London, Ontario, Mr. Latta first became a school teacher and later graduated from Ontario School of Arts. He was author of several books, among them "Latta's Drawing Book," used by Ontario schools for many years.

In 1905 he responded to the call of the west, and homesteaded near Govan, Saskatchewan. Two years later he established the *The Govan Prairie News* which he published until 1929.

He was first elected to the Saskatchewan legislative assembly in 1912 and continued to be re-elected until 1929 when he was defeated along with the other members of the Gardiner government in the landslide election of the Anderson Conservative government.

While a member of the legislature he served as minister of highways, minister of education, minister of municipal affairs and provincial secretary for terms of varying lengths. He was finally appointed commissioner of the Bureau of Publications for ten years previous to retirement in 1944.

Mr. Latta was a man of deep integrity and a friend of all, for he remained a common man, regardless of the title "Honorable", which was officially carried in front of his name for so many years.

"Couldn't be anything else but," he said time and again. "A common man I was born. A common man I will die."

No other words could more fittingly describe his personality. He was indeed a "common man", in the very best sense of the term.

He died in 1945 at his home in Regina.

SAMUEL NATHAN WYNN, LL.D.

Beginning at the age of 14 to learn the operation of a typesetting machine, the experiences of Samuel Nathan Wynn, LL.D., in the field of weekly journalism, leading progressively to manager, editor and finally owner, equipped him with a storehouse of knowledge which he freely contributed to the promotion and progress of weekly newspapers individually and through the medium of national and provincial associations.

On coming west in 1914 he encountered the many problems and difficulties common to the struggling weekly newspaper business at that time.

With determination, he wrestled with each perplexing situation as it arose, until he had overcome and tucked the solution away in his well-indexed memory bank.

These problems included almost every one that could confront a weekly newspaper. All required careful assessment and analysis if the troubles were to be surmounted. Experience, the best teacher, provided Sam with a great store of knowledge and understanding, an asset which he freely shared with other publishers when called upon.

Early in his career, he sought to become familiar with others' experiences; hence his first attendance at the 1905 convention of Western Canada Press Association in Winnipeg. From then on, he rarely missed a provincial or national convention.

With a storehouse of information, he was frequently called upon to speak at these gatherings where his unostentatious platform presence, quiet mannerisms and his down-to-earth presentations were greatly appreciated. Sam always called a spade a spade, and subjects of his addresses were always to the point.

As early as 1910 he addressed the Western Canada Press Association's annual meeting on the apprenticeship question in weekly offices.

At that time printers in the cities were scarce. Employers there drew most of their help as graduates from country newspaper offices, but the latter were finding it hard to engage apprentices.

Sam was most outspoken. He urged the tidying up of the dirty, dingy country printing shops which provided little appeal to bright, intelligent boys which the industry needed so badly.

The range of topics he was invited to discuss included such as plant management, shop methods, editorial writing, reporting, office routine, advertising promotion, public relations. His presentations were of value not only to the tyro, but also to those more advanced in the profession and vocation.

The Saskatchewan Press Association held a short course in journalism at the University of Saskatchewan in 1920, the first of many such courses conducted over the intervening years. Sam was chosen to preside at it.

During the era of the Famous Four Sams he was most active in building up the standards of Saskatchewan weekly newspapers through his leadership in promoting better news coverage, improved typography, presswork and business methods. His influence had much to do with the general improvement in the quality of many of the provinces weekly newspapers, and hence a greater degree of local acceptance and respect in their circulation areas.

Chapter 21

PRESS ASSOCIATIONS

The Western Canada Press Association was organized in 1896. Looking backward, this action can be rated as a bold, unusual one at so early a date in the rural development of the prairies. It is the more noteworthy that it preceded the formation of all other types of business groups. Even Boards of Trade were unknown and unthought of in those pioneer times.

The history of this association is impossible to assemble in other than a sketchy manner. No one knows where its records may be stored, if indeed they still exist.

Its first members whose memories might have provided at least the basic facts of the story have long since passed from the scene.

It is somewhat incongruous that one of the few bits of WCPA history available is a record of one privilege which weekly newspaper publishers had during the later 1890s and early 1900s, which incidentally, in one respect, gave them equal status with clergymen.

During those years, annual travel passes on the Canadian Pacific Railway were issued to publishers on request. These were in the form of a card which had only to be shown to a passenger train conductor to secure free transportation.

The railway company did not consider this practice an act of charity or purchase of editorial bias on its behalf. It looked upon every weekly newspaper as a factor in stimulating colonization.

It calculated that every new family moving into the urban or rural area it served added an average of $250 a year to its revenues from freight charges on the movement of commodities and grain shipped over its lines.

Following the discontinuing of these annual passes, transportation to publishers was issued on a somewhat loose "contra account" basis. Still later this plan was done away with. For some years now editors and publishers have been paying cash for rail transportation just the same as any other traveller.

In regard to membership, the Western Canada Press Association would appear to have been in a strong position at least by 1912 when it had 250 newspapers on its roster.

The territory it embraced extended from Fort William and Port Arthur, Ontario, across Manitoba and through the North West Territories to the British Columbia boundary. Its northern rim had no geographical marking other than a flexible line determined by the location of the most northerly newspaper offices.

Membership in this association included daily and weekly newspapers, trade and other magazines. There were very few of the latter. In this respect it was similar to the national Canadian Press Association with which it was loosely affiliated.

A press report of its annual convention held in Fort William in 1912 stated that only 50 out of the total member-ship of 250 were present. Disappointment was expressed by the officers at this small turnout as preparations had been made to play host to 100.

Some surprise can be expressed at this attitude on the part of the officers, because actually the country weekly news-papers, which made up the majority of the members, were not exactly in a thriving financial position; they were also suffering from a scarcity of well-trained printers.

Then, as well, time of travel to and from the convention plus four days of sessions, totalled up to as much as ten days for many publishers in the more westerly areas, much too long to be absent from their business activities.

It was not at all out of order for the main discussions to center on the prevalence of unprofitable advertising rates, low job printing prices and the shortage of capable printers.

It is a matter of more than passing interest to note that

even in those pioneer days of 1912, a young newspaperman from Yorkton, Saskatchewan, S. N. Wynn, had attracted notice for his sound assessment of problems common to the profession, and his opinions as to how they might be solved.

Accordingly, he was elected second vice-president and in 1913 was given the second boost up the presidential ladder by being advanced to the first vice-presidency.

His failure to reach the topmost position was brought about by the organization of the Saskatchewan Press Association in 1915 and the break-up of the Western Canada Press Association to make way for provincial associations. But Sam Wynn became the first secretary of the Saskatchewan Press Association. W. G. Cates, of *The Moose Jaw Times* was its first president.

No records are available of the short-lived SPA, due to action at the national level.

The Canadian Press Association with a national membership roll was divided into three sections—weekly and daily newspapers and magazines. Each of these had slightly differing interests. Each had its own slate of officers and managed its own affairs.

One of these groups was the Canadian Weekly Newspapers Association. In 1917 it withdrew from affiliation with the Canadian Press Association to become an entirely independent organization.

It followed that in the same year the Saskatchewan Press Association became the Saskatchewan Division, Canadian Weekly Newspapers Association with Cameron R. McIntosh of *The North Battleford News* as president and S. N. Wynn of *The Yorkton Enterprise* continuing as secretary.

It continued with that designation until 1961 when it was incorporated under Saskatchewan Benevolent Societies Act as the Saskatchewan Press Association. This move was made not because a lawyer-publisher some years previously had pointed out that the Saskatchewan Division, SWNA had no more legal standing than a small town amateur baseball club, but because of new business activities which the association was assuming.

(For convenience, from this point on, The Saskatchewan Division CWNA will be referred to as Saskatchewan Press Association.)

Prior to the 1920s, the requirements to operate a weekly publishing and printing business in a financially successful manner were not commonly understood or practiced. Most of the weekly publishers had been just printers in the back shop before moving into the front office. They lacked office and accounting experience and also, to a degree, reporting and editorial experience.

As a matter of fact, few knew how to calculate their costs of advertising space and commercial printing. Prices of these were set to some extent by guesswork, by prices charged by others or by an erratic compliance with suggested prices compiled by a supply house, or on rare occasions by press associations.

In some cases the prices at which advertising space was sold were so low that the publisher simply could not make even a decent wage for himself.

During the first few years, the active officers of the Saskatchewan Press Association centered their efforts on stimulating better edited and better printed newspapers. Its conventions featured discussions led by competent speakers dealing with such topics as "The Business End of a Weekly Newspaper;" "Editorial, its Value, Place, Scope and Purpose in a Weekly Newspaper;" "The Local Newspaper from the Subscriber's Point of View" and others in similar vein.

In 1920 the first short course or work shops were carried out. These have been repeated at different times during the ensuing years.

While this practical instruction did much to raise publishing and business standards among weekly publishers, one member was convinced in his own mind that the entire membership had fallen into a self-satisfied rut with new opportunities being ignored.

At the association convention held in October, 1923, members were jarred out of their complacency by Sam Dornan, an outspoken Irishman who had purchased *The Alameda Dispatch* a year or two previously. He declared the whole organization was an innocuous group with an unattained purpose. The accompanying tirade was of historic importance, emphasized and colored by a resonant Irish brogue.

Almost before he had finished and had time to sit down, he was elected secretary-manager. The convention delegates, irritated to varying degrees, or maybe happy to load a burden on someone else, voiced a common thought. It was "alright, now let's see what you can do about it."

Sam proved that something could be done about it and he was quickly supported by Sam N. Wynn of Yorkton, Hon. Sam J. Latta of Govan and Sam R. Moore of Swift Current.

This group, the "Four Sams", provided the stimulus that was to bring the association to its richest period of growth, status and influence.

Dornan's initial plan was to bring every weekly newspaper in Saskatchewan into membership in the association, and through his office providing a service to government departments and specific types of business.

His office would contract to place the advertising required by these clients in member newspapers. This relieved the advertiser of a great deal of detailed office routine having only one invoice to pay, instead of many as he would when dealing directly with each individual newspaper.

Dornan first deducted the current rate of advertising agency commission from the publishers' invoices. The net balance was then remitted to them. The commission deductions were applied in payment of membership fees with any surplus left being placed in the association's treasury to be used for operating expenses.

Eligible newspaper publishers who were not members quickly became such in order to secure additional advertising.

It was a plan that satisfied everyone. In addition it created increased interest in all of the association's activities, resulting in larger attendance at conventions where capable speakers advised on better business methods, higher ethical standards, improvement in newspaper typography, news reporting and editorials.

Not the least benefit received from the association's annual conventions was the social intermingling between delegates, their wives and people in high places of government and business. These personal contacts broadened mutual understanding and business relationships both within as well as without the circle of those actively engaged in the news-paper field.

These contacts made it much easier to establish standard practices among publishers, particularly in the area of national advertising, at a time when advertising agencies were becoming impatient with a number of unnecessary variations in contracts imposed by some publishers, and the dilatory manner in which their accounts were treated.

A fuller recognition of the influence of the weekly press on its constituency by provincial and federal governments resulted in more advertising from these sources.

The association decided that action should be taken to interview agencies in Eastern Canada to acquaint them with the blanket coverage of the rural areas offered by the weekly press of Saskatchewan.

To carry out this project, Secretary-manager Dornan travelled 6500 miles in the year 1927. There were few advertis-ing agency executives who did not hear his presentation of the association's claim for a greater share of the national adver-tiser's budget.

The home front was not being ignored. Over a period of several years, Sam R. Moore led many forums at the associa-tion conventions, designed to improve the all-around stand-ards of the weekly newspapers. By 1932, many of these were winning awards in all classes of the Canadian Weekly News-papers Association annual competitions.

Never before or since have the weekly newspapers of Saskatchewan, as a whole, operated under more favorable conditions. They had reached a pinnacle of influence through self-improvement of their services. They had the most complete rural readership of all publications, a condition which many national advertisers took advantage of.

Advertising rates in general had been set to provide a reasonable profit to the publisher.

The province was well covered with the largest number of weeklies of all time. Most plants had been modernized and were well-equipped; there were also more well-trained printers. The visions of Sam Dornan and a few other progressives had become realities.

By 1929, there were 159 weekly newspapers in Saskatchewan and every one eligible was a member of Saskatchewan Press Association.

At the 1932 convention President Andrew King presented the association with a gavel of historic import. It was made of oak wood from the old Hudson's Bay Company steamboat, the *Marquis*. In the earliest pioneer days of the west, the vessel sailed a regular schedule through spring, summer and autumn on the Saskatchewan River from the head of Lake Winnipeg to Battleford—a route that was then the main avenue of traffic into the west. During the 1885 rebellion the *Marquis* carried troops to Prince Albert.

With the building of railroads across the prairies, the river route was discontinued. Its days of usefulness ended, the *Marquis* was finally moored on the north bank of the river downstream from Prince Albert. Later it was partially destroyed by fire of unknown origin and after half a century was finally dismantled.

The gavel, which carried an appropriate inscription, was received on behalf of the association by Vice-President John Scott.

All weekly newspapers felt acutely the impact of the depression years of the 1930s. Their owners fared worse than most other types of business. Dealers in foodstuffs, machinery and other necessities required in farming continued to make sales even if they were much less than normal volume.

In the sense of being a commodity satisfying an absolute need, a weekly newspaper did not qualify. Subscribers and advertisers could get along without patronizing it—and many did. Yet only a very few publishers in the entire province received even the smallest measure of government relief.

Throughout the depression they generally felt a responsibility to ignore the discouraging financial picture and kept their columns more or less free from reference to dismal economic conditions. Their news reporting and editorials carried overtones designed to keep to the fore the friendly, neighborly atmosphere which was one of the richest by-products of the depression. In this regard it is fitting to recall an editorial carried by the *Regina Leader-Post* in 1935:

"Saskatchewan weekly newspapers have all been maintained despite the drubbing the province has received, a harder one than has been had to be borne in almost any other part of Canada. During the five years of it the weekly publishers have stuck to their job and have kept their chins up. They have been busily engaged in serving the public and the community and at the same time trying to make an honest dollar for the business."

By 1938 it was noted that several weeklies had amalgamated with others and members as a whole were suffering from the strenuous times. though some had moved their offices to new locations, mainly in more northerly towns, which seemed to hold out promise of greater security.

1939 annual convention was held in the dismal atmosphere of war time. President Jim Greenblat had a timely, and as always, a prophetic message, which in part, was as follows:

"In my opinion we face a long, terrible struggle against the forces of evil which will take every bit of material and human resource that we can muster and we might as well face the situation now . . . I hope that by resolution you will indicate how the weekly publishers of this province stand ready to co-operate with our government in this period of stress. They have a tremendous burden to carry and we should give our undivided support, eschewing politics and immaterial things to attain the goal of once again having a world which may be free from threat and aggression. . . . It is gratifying indeed to have noted the admirable restraint which has been exercised by Saskatchewan weeklies in handling the amenities of this war. As a matter of fact it has brought forth editorial comment from the daily press already."

When in 1944, Robert Moore, of *The Swift Current Sun* was elected president it was the first occasion that a son of a former president was chosen for that office. His father, Sam P. Moore, had held the position 16 years previously. In a true sense it symbolized the rise of the second generation, now carrying on the businesses the fathers had established.

Since that year, four sons of former presidents of the Saskatchewan Press Association have been elected to the presidency namely:

Stirling King, 1951-52, *Estevan Mercury*, son of Andrew King (1931-32); Irwin McIntosh, 1957-58, *North Battleford News Optimist*, son of Cameron McIntosh (1918-1920); Joseph Ashfield, 1967-68, *Whitewood Herald*, son of Walter Ashfield (1930-31); W. Morphy, 1968-69, *Biggar Independent*, son of W. T. Morphy (1936-37).

During the 1944 convention an incident occurred which slightly cooled a continuation of happy relationships between provincial governments and association members which had existed for a third of a century. While speaking at a luncheon tendered the convention delegates by a paper wholesale house, Hon. C. M. Fines rather plainly intimated that the government of which he was a part was not going to let newspaper publishers push it around. Several of the delegates left the banquet room while he was speaking.

The exigencies of wartime caused the 1945 convention scheduled for Regina, to be cancelled. A conference was called instead but the hotel accommodation was restricted to 40 persons and 20 rooms. It was strictly a business gathering. Social functions were eliminated. One resolution quite vividly revealed one segment of prevailing restrictions. It urged all users of paper in any form to adopt measures ensuring the utmost conservation of this commodity. With the price of newsprint escalating, as well as other production costs, most weeklies began raising their subscription price to $2 per year.

In 1946, the CCF government passed the Apprenticeship Act, setting forth conditions under which apprentices to the printing trade could be trained in weekly newspaper offices. The Act specified the nature of contract they would enter into. Due to the scarcity of trained printers this move was at first looked upon with much favor by the publishers.

However, by 1948, there were only 10 apprentices in all of the weekly offices, which indicated that the regulations were not exactly in tune with current conditions. Representations were made to the government for changes to be made in the act.

First, it was pointed out that wages to be paid apprentices under the provisions of the act at the rate of 42 per cent of journeyman's scale was too high for a technical trade requiring a large amount of personal instruction and supervision by top-salaried journeymen. The second claim was that the clause requiring an apprentice to be sent to a trade school for a stated period each year created too much hardship on the employer.

It was also reported members had found that apprentices would leave after a few months to go to other offices offering more money, and nothing could be gained by taking action against the apprentice for breach of contract.

The Apprenticeship Board lowered the rate of wages and removed the clause requiring the apprentice's attendance at a trade school. No remedy could be produced covering breach of contract. The act became a dead issue.

For almost a quarter of a century, governments had played hide-and-seek with liquor, wine and beer advertising in newspapers. As early as 1925 the Saskatchewan government proposed to prohibit all such publicity, but press representation caused it to refrain from carrying out its proposals. Again in 1932 the Saskatchewan Liquor Board placed a ban on advertising, but in 1933 the restriction was lifted with respect to beer and wine.

As a wartime measure, advertising of liquors, wines and beer was prohibited by the federal government in 1942. This action was later amended to permit advertising of all of these products but pictures of drinking scenes were banned in such advertising. Some advertisers promoted Victory Bond campaigns in their campaigns.

Finally, in 1947, all this vacillating came to an end in Saskatchewan when the CCF government prohibited all types of liquor, wine and beer advertising in provincial publications. It justified its action by stating it was fulfilling a pre-election promise.

Total revenue to all provincial weekly newspapers at that time from liquor advertising averaged about $4000 per month or, roughly, $30 per month per newspaper. There were a few weeklies which for years had refused to accept any contracts for this type of advertising.

In 1947, S. J. Dornan resigned as secretary-manager of the association after 25 years of outstanding service. He was presented with a Henderson painting, an inscribed salver, and an illuminated address.

The following year it seemed most fitting that he should receive recognition of his contribution to weekly newspaperdom, provincially and nationally, by the University of Saskatchewan, which conferred on him the honorary degree of Doctor of Laws. For similar service, the same University honored S. N. Wynn, of Yorkton with the same degree in 1955.

Following Mr. Dornan's resignation, the association entered a span of years during which, for various reasons, the succeeding secretary-managers, each served far shorter terms of office.

Walter Ashfield of Grenfell filled the position from 1947 till 1953, when ill health forced him to retire. His recording of proceedings and reports was meticulous in detail; and in other ways he carried out his duties with great distinction.

John A. Vopni of Davidson succeeded Mr. Ashfield, and he closely followed the admirable style of Mr. Ashfield.

In 1959, Mr. Vopni resigned, and Jessie M. Dales of Herbert bravely accepted the responsible post when no male member appeared willing to assume the task. Mrs. Dales continued until the appointment of Joe E. Brown in 1967.

Sam Dornan's name again appeared in the records in 1949, when he became the first honorary life member of the Saskatchewan Press Association. That same year, the association and the Saskatchewan Department of Education discussed the possibility of having printing instruction added to the provincial school curriculum. In 1950, a plan for Grades 9 and 10 students was set up. This was a two-year course providing one high school credit. Considerable interest was shown at the time, and the association recommended that the course be extended into Grade 11, and include study of linotype operation and news reporting. But due to lack of applications and interest on the part of pupils, the entire scheme dwindled away during the next few years.

The names of three publishers prominent in Saskatchewan weekly newspaper circles were given permanent recognition in 1950. Three lakes in the North West Territories were named after P. C. Laurie, S. R. Moore and Donald C. Dunbar.

For the visit of Princess Elizabeth and the Duke of Edinburgh in 1952, President Stirling King was accredited as special press correspondent on the royal train as it crossed Canada. Robert Moore of Swift Current, vice-president of the Canadian Weekly Newspapers Association, was also a member of the royal tour press corps.

The atmosphere of the 1952 convention indicated that the weekly newspaper business had improved its economic standing which had been seriously impaired during the depression and war years. The publishers and their wives were finding conditions less frustrating and demanding. At least they had time to play a bit. That convention had the largest attendance in the history of the association with a total of 250 members, wives and guests.

Yet, it was only a few years later the pinch of changing business conditions began to take its toll. Small towns had begun to get smaller while printing and publishing costs were rising.

In 1954, there were 158 weeklies in Saskatchewan of which 135 were members of the association. These papers were issued from 98 offices. In many cases, publishers continued to edit their own papers, but had the printing done by another shop. This trend continued, and in 1955, membership had dropped to 109, with issuing offices down to 94.

In the face of these conditions, the Saskatchewan Press Association's financial position was quite normal, with $1300 worth of government bonds among its assets. Additional bonds in the amount of $3000 were bought in 1957 from commissions earned on advertising in 1955 Saskatchewan's Jubilee Year supplement used by member newspapers.

For the first time in the association's history, politics quite openly reared its head within the membership at a district meeting held at Swift Current in 1962. It could only be recognized as an expression of a changing attitude similar to that which had developed in the thinking of all people on the prairies within a decade.

At that meeting, a resolution was passed unanimously. It read as follows:

"Whereas there is a growing tendency of the CCF-NDP government of Saskatchewan, which represents a minority of electors, to implement more and more socialism into its operations in opposition to a majority of the electors, therefore it is strongly recommended by the editors and publishers attending this zone meeting of the Saskatchewan Weekly Newspapers Association in Swift Current, April 15, 1962, that they take a firm stand in support of the free and private enterprise system at the time of the next provincial election."

When the resolution was presented at the association's annual convention in Regina it was accompanied by a statement outlining the reasons for its adoption at the zone meeting.

The main argument presented was "it may not be true that the government is deliberately embarked on a program to restrict our freedom but it is true that the incessant demands and pressures brought to bear on it by people seeking further social and other types of service is strengthening the government's position at the expense of the people's freedom. It is this situation that the weekly press should attack."

Objections to the resolution were voiced by various delegates. They mainly expressed the belief that decision to support or reject any type of political philosophy should be left to the individual and not taken on an association basis. The resolution was defeated by a vote of 33 to 3.

Ever-increasing wage levels began to be felt by weekly newspapers during the early 1960s. Those published in the smaller towns and with smaller circulations were most severely affected.

Combined with the reduction of rural population which was gradually taking place, high costs resulted in the closing down of retail and other kinds of business. Mounting production costs began to place an ever-mounting economic pressure on all weeklies.

Yet it is somewhat incongruous to find that while one group of publishers was suffering from these conditions, another smaller group, was enjoying an increasing and more profitable volume of business to strengthen their economic position and influence in their respective areas. These were in the larger towns with favorable geographical location in which there was a greater centralization of businesses of all kinds.

These favored newspapers were thus able to expand their plants by adding such modern equipment as tape operated linotypes and rotary web presses, enabling them more easily to combat increased costs.

But for the smaller weeklies it was only a matter of time until some went out of business. Others however began to side-step some of the high production costs by having their issues printed by neighboring offices. In this connection, the use of the offset process of printing, eased the situation to some extent. The technique made it possible to replace a highly skilled linotype operator with a typist of average talent, with a saving in wages of up to 50 per cent.

With radio and television capturing more and more of the business formerly placed in weekly newspapers by national advertisers, the weeklies in a short decade had lost a substantial amount of revenue.

To offset this loss in some measure, the directors of the Saskatchewan Weekly Newspapers Association decided this gap could be partially filled by certain types of business and institutions requiring coverage only within the province or within lesser local areas. To promote this, the association decided in 1967 to engage a full-time secretary-manager and set up a full-time office in Regina. Joe A. C. Brown, an experienced advertising solicitor was chosen for this position.

The office provided all the services of an advertising agency, including the placing of advertising, public relations, copy writing, purchase of printing, news releases and checking, all handled on a one order, one invoice and one cheque plan for the advertisers. This was a much broader service than that instituted by Sam J. Dornan, and carried on by his successors. An ever-increasing volume of business being placed indicates that this office is providing a service filling a need.

Over many years, the SWNA workshops held with regularity have aided the weekly newspapermen to keep in touch with and abreast of rapidly changing conditions within the profession. The word "workshop" is most appropriate. The members attending are serious in their participation.

Conventions continue, as always, to be the happy event of each year with breakfasts, luncheons and dinners providing social contacts amid the two-day business sessions.

It was at the 1966 convention that a new classification of recognition was instituted when Alex C. Cameron was awarded the honorary title of Printer's Devil No. 1, in a delightful little ceremony. Alex had just retired from The Saskatchewan Wheat Pool, after serving 15 years as director of publicity. It was a position which put him in close touch with the weekly publishers of Saskatchewan who appreciated the efficient and understanding manner in which he placed the Pool's publicity and news releases.

In 1969, there were 118 weekly newspapers in Saskatchewan. For the reason that some could not meet the news, typographical and circulation standards set by the association, membership stood at 89. These were being produced in only 75 plants, with 26 printed by the offset process. The publishers of four, operate two-unit offset presses using roll newsprint and printing and folding eight-page newspaper sections at speeds of 4000 or more copies per hour. These machines are installed in plants of *The Assiniboia Times, Biggar Independent, Lloydminster Times* and *Weyburn Review*.

What of the future of weekly newspapers in Western Canada? There is little doubt but that the factors which first stabilized the operation of them have almost completely disappeared. This is particularly true in the wheatland areas.

Dwindling rural population, the fading away of neighborly intimacies, the broadened news scope of electronic communications, plus a more materialistic economic outlook have weakened the links between the weeklies and the farm homes to a marked degree.

Almost every change in technology, and in industrial and social life has narrowed the field of profitable operation of country weekly newspapers.

But no matter how the entire weekly newspaper business is challenged by adversity, it will remain a distinct and useful contribution to the way of life of the western prairies.

Chapter 22

THE MOOSOMIN WORLD-SPECTATOR

N ewspaper history in the North West Territories began with the publication of *The Battleford Press*. Alone in the field, the newspaper acquired prestige not equalled by later publications.

Yet of all the 16 newspapers which began publication previous to 1890, in the area now Saskatchewan, not one of them provides a more colorful story than *The Moosomin Courier* and its successor *The Moosomin World-Spectator*.

This may be due to the lack of detailed records regarding most of the others. *The Courier's* long history continues as an unbroken and authenticated chain from its beginning

Established in 1884, *The Courier* reflected the stirring days of the 1885 rebellion; pictured the unusually bitter political animosities which developed in Moosomin for a time, as well as the pioneer life of rural settlement involving earnest, hard-working and even adventurous people, with some British remittance men thrown in, creating within a small area an unusual community.

It saw a few unhappy incidents. One man lost a finger operating the press while printing the very first issue of *The Courier*. There were the anxieties of lean years. Competition at times brought worry to the owners.

Maybe they smiled just a little when the two editors of the opposition newspaper absconded, each taking with him the contents of the till.

The Courier finally became *The World-Spectator*, an event preceded by a money-borrowing experience which would rarely, if ever be duplicated in modern times.

During the years from 1884 until the present, some 16

different owners and editors were involved with it and its competitors—a high average in Saskatchewan newspaper history.

Because of *The Courier's* close association with the events of the pioneer days and the part it played in the early history of the North West Territories, it is not at all surprising that in August, 1966, the Canadian Broadcasting Corporation presented a full hour program devoted to the newspaper, based mainly on its issue of May 7, 1885, one of the very few early copies still in existence. Its front page carried a news dispatch dated April 30, from Camp Fish Creek, dealing with action in the Riel Rebellion.

The Courier was the sixth weekly newspaper to start in the North West Territories. The first, of course, was *The Battleford Herald,* in 1878; the second, *The Prince Albert Times and Saskatchewan Review,* 1882-1912; the third, *The Regina Leader,* 1883-1916; the fourth was *The Moose Jaw News,* which was published April 27, 1883, to some unrecorded date in 1885; the fifth was *The Qu'Appelle Record* which began publication in 1883 with its last issue dated April 11, 1884.

Incidentally, all daily newspapers presently being published in Saskatchewan, began as weeklies.

In any case, *The Courier* and its final successor, *The World-Spectator,* holds the record for Saskatchewan and Alberta among all others as the weekly newspaper published without interruption for the longest period of years from one location.

As a matter of fact, of all the others which began during the 1880s (with one exception, *The Indian Head News,* only one week younger than *The World-Spectator*) have ceased publication, including those which moved into the daily field.

The Courier was first issued as a weekly, but from April till late July or early August, 1885, it was issued daily. Carrying news of the rebellion, it sold readily at the railway station to passengers travelling west on the trains.

The page size of the first issue was about 9 by 12 inches. It had six pages of closely-set type. Bert McKay, now publisher of *The World-Spectator* writes: "As far as I know, there are no copies in existence of *The Daily Courier*, though the Archives might have some pieces."

It does not require much imagination to visualize the eagerness with which the beginning of *The Courier* was greeted, and the impact it made. The town was far away from others where newspapers were published.

Moosomin then was barely 300 in population. There was little settlement north or south of the town, but *The Courier* did circulate in towns east and west along the CPR main line.

Its founders were D. M. Nulty, G. F. Leaper and Thomas Beer. It was Leaper who had his finger taken off by the printing press. Nulty stayed only a short time with Leaper leaving not long after.

The Courier was carried on for 10 years by Beer when he sold it to O. Smith, who changed its name to *The Spectator*.

A second paper, *The Moosomin Journal and Assiniboia News* was started in 1892. It lasted for only 30 weeks.

As *The Spectator* became a staunch and wordy supporter of the Liberal party, the local Conservatives became annoyed, so formed a company and began publishing *The World*. The vice-president of this company was John McGuire, a furniture factory owner who made many of the old benches in the Saskatchewan legislative building in Regina.

Because of absconding editors and other problems, the company decided to sell the business to two men of the opposition *Spectator* staff. They were Oscar Bretz and Herbert Shuart, who had no cash but had an idea where they might get it.

They went to a nearby town to present their plea to a man known to loan money providing he received a rather stiff rate of interest. They found this gentleman ill, so their request was made to him under somewhat adverse conditions, as he lay in bed, After hearing their case he simply reached under the bed, pulled out a metal box and counted out the $2800 needed for the newspaper purchase.

A few years later, Bretz and Shuart were asked by Smith to buy his paper. When the deal was made he asked that the name *Spectator* be preserved. This was agreed upon, so on

Nov. 2, 1910, the first issue of *The Moosomin World-Spectator* rolled off the press.

This rather striking name continues to be well-known in Canadian newspaper circles.

Shuart died in 1936 and his share was purchased by Bert McKay. Then with the death of Bretz in 1941, McKay became sole owner.

With the decision to undertake publication of newspapers in several towns, McKay Publications was formed in 1966, with Bert McKay as president; John Meen (a local boy who was editor of *The Renfrew Ont. Mercury* for five years, as vice-president and editor, and Mrs. Roberta McKay as secretary-treasurer.

The World-Spectator was hand set until 1937 as the two old-time printers had failed to accept the advantages provided by the coming of the mechanical age. In that year the first modernization took place leading up to the present highly efficient operation.

A flash-back giving a clear picture of certain aspects of life in Moosomin in the 1880s was uncovered in 1966 with the demolition of the old frame building which first housed *The Courier*.

Several samples of printing were discovered, pasted between the uprights of the shop walls. When the inside of the walls had originally been boarded up later, these samples were kept in a good state of preservation as well as being hidden until the wrecking gang went to work.

Two of the samples were posters. One advertised an 1885 Dominion Day sports day at Moosomin. No less than $200 in prizes were offered—a lot of cash in those days. Events were foot races, hurdles, horse racing, quoits, tug-of-war and baseball with a $10 prize.

The second poster revealed more of the social atmosphere of the times. It was advertising the grand opening of the bar and billiard room at the Queen's Hotel. This was a frame hostelry put up in a hurry when the Canadian Pacific Railway reached Moosomin. It was the fifth hotel in town.

Those were the days of the "open bar:"customers had to stand up while drinking. There were no chairs or tables.

The bar itself, or counter, over which liquor was served, was high enough for the average drinker to lean on comfortably, while a rail about six inches above the floor was a resting place for tired feet, one foot at a time.

Large spittoons were there for the convenience of those addicted to chewing Macdonald plug tobbacco. Accurate expectoration was a greatly admired skill.

Dining rooms were incidental to the hotel business, yet provided a much-needed service for farmers who required a full day to drive to town, conduct their business and still get back to their farms, preferably in daylight.

Restaurants were rare places in the small towns until the coming of the Chinese. Children ate free, while 25c would buy a full meal, including extra helpings. The bars, of course, subsidized the dining rooms.

The weekly newspaper is something very special to millions of Canadian people. It is an intimate, informal vehicle for information of common interest. It is as personal as a man's pipe or a woman's handbag; and it is as indispensable in a wide awake community as once was the traditional Town Crier.

—PROF. GLEN HANCOCK,
King's University, Halifax, N.S.

Chapter 23

PAPERS AND PUBLISHERS

Over 500 weekly newspapers have been started in Saskatchewan since Patrick Gammie Laurie began issuing the historic *Battleford Press* in 1878.

The number of publishers involved is impossible to determine with any degree of accuracy, but it has been suggested there has been at least 1500. That calculation is based on an average of three to each newspaper. The true figure could be more than that.

Some of the newspapers have had as many as twelve different publishers. More have had as many as seven and eight and there are very few that have not been owned by at least three over a period of years.

It is to be expected that within a group of such dimension are to be found a wide range of personalities with varying talents, objectives and ambitions.

Even in the smallest towns were to be found men—yes, even women—who were not only capable business people but who had a keen sense of news values and the ability to report the news of their communities in skilful manner. They produced newspapers which in every respect were much superior to many published in larger centers and more heavily populated areas.

It was but natural that the level of talent occasionally ran to the other extreme. Some publishers turned out weeklies with poor news coverage, careless typography and slovenly presswork. Obviously, these persons kept drifting into the smaller centers where their newspapers were the first to cease publication under the unrelenting pressures of changing business conditions.

Yet there was one thing the entire group had in common, and that was active participation in community affairs. Publishers and editors of weekly newspapers have provided a higher percentage of mayors, overseers, aldermen, councillors, school trustees, presidents of Chambers of Commerce and office holders in all sorts of community welfare associations than any other occupational or professional group.

In the more specialized segment of newspaperdom, Saskatchewan weekly publishers had a liberal share of presidencies in the Canadian Weekly Newspaper Association; many were recognized—again in rich ratio—with honorary life memberships.

Some newspapers in Saskatchewan have continued under family ownership for two and even three generations. Others have been carried on by wives following the decease of their husbands.

A few have been operated by one person for many years, though none can challenge the record of John Scott of Whitewood who for 55 years published *The Whitewood Herald* from the time he purchased it until his retirement.

There were weeklies—now in the larger cities and towns—which in size of circulation and number of pages per issue, merely kept pace with the gradual growth of their home towns.

Only one, *The Swift Current Sun*, broke this pattern, following its purchase from Sam P. Moore by his son Bob, Jim Greenblat and Mahlon Hutchison in 1937.

Here was a trio of top talent, with much experience in office management and policy, news reporting, editorial writing and mechanical equipment.

They first envisioned Swift Current as a business center for a large area. With a carefully selected corps of correspondents over a wide region they increased *Sun* circulation to more than three times that which they had purchased—an increase outstripping the plodding growth of their small city.

This rapid business expansion could be credited to the specialized talents of the three owners. Bob Moore knew the mechanics of the business from front office to composing room. Jim Greenblat had already established a fine reputation both as news and editorial writer. Mahlon Hutchison was skilled in producing good typography, page make-up and presswork.

Only one example of the objectivity and originality of these three men is needed to picture the manner in which they placed *The Sun* in its enviable position.

The issue of Feb. 17, 1942, had a startling front page headed "The Deutschlander" with articles by-lined with the names of Goebels, Hitler and other top-ranking Nazis.

It was ostensibly a take-over of Swift Current by the Nazis. In reality, the whole thing was conceived for the purpose of publicizing the Second Victory Loan. It brought national recognition, resulting in telegrams from government officials, newspapers and many men prominent in public eye.

A little later, Greenblat and Moore bought Hutchison's interest and on Greenblat's retirement in 1957, Moore and Dave Belbeck bought his shares in the company.

Here once more special talent was present, Belbeck being a "professional" writer with contributions to many top magazines to his credit.

By 1966, Dave and Bob had increased the circulation of *The Sun* to over 7300. They had a staff of 28 employees.

Dave Belbeck's news stories in *The Sun* were reprinted in various publications. One which caused an unusual stir was about a man who became ill after drinking slough water. Following an X-ray examination, a local doctor allegedly found a lizard in the patient's stomach; *The Sun* printed a picture to prove it. Dave later confessed it was pure fiction, but the story did *The Sun* no harm.

A great majority of weekly newspaper publishers entered the field through the "back shop" by first learning the printing trade in country offices. As 'teenagers, they had decided on this course.

It is therefore of more than casual interest to find a few who, on reaching middle age without the slightest notion of ever becoming printers or publishers, became suddenly involved in those vocations. Such as Tom Kearns of *The Kipling Citizen*.

Following his discharge from the army at the close of the Second World War, he was at loose ends and unable to make a decision as to his future occupation.

He found himself often in the company of Walter Ash-field of Grenfell. He was continually in and out of Ashfield's newspaper office where he would meet other newspapermen from nearby places.

Tom tells of how he suddenly became aware of the warm fraternal spirit that existed among these men. This observation led to the decision that he would be perfectly happy in the newspaper business.

After spending a year with Walter getting a grounding in the art of printing and newspaper writing, he purchased *The Kipling Citizen* in 1946. Since then he has enjoyed participation in his chosen profession, his community activities, and in spreading good cheer on every side.

He has a fine gift for topical writing in gossipy fashion, and fills a weekly column titled "Tomitorials." Asked why he chose such an artificial designation, he simply says: "Those paragraphs are my editorials, but my name is not Ed."

E. J. Brunyanski, owner of the *Wakaw Recorder*, was somewhat similarily attracted to the weekly newspaper business though under different circumstances. He had a vagrant life during the depression years, riding freight trains back and forth, picking up odd jobs here and there between British Columbia lumber camps and Ontario tobacco fields.

During the Second World War, he served five years with the Royal Canadian Air Force as a mechanic, but found himself in idleness following his discharge. He yearned for some occupation in which he might hope to be satisfied and which could provide him with a fair degree of security.

One day he was in a printing office where he watched a man setting type by hand. He was instantly fascinated, and on learning that the Wakaw newspaper was for sale, just went and bought it, without any knowledge of the printing trade or business administration.

He has never regretted his hasty action. When he took over *The Times* in 1948, its circulation was around 350. Today it is six times that figure. His progress from an untrained printer to a highly successful newspaperman holding high office in newspaper associations, is quite remarkable.

A lucky encounter steered him into profession commensurate with his talents.

* * *

The Journal, published at Humboldt, Sask., has an unusual heritage. It has been published continuously since its inception by three generations of one family—the Telfers.

This constitutes a record for the greatest number of consecutive years a weekly newspaper has been published in Saskatchewan by one family. In fact the same could also be claimed as a Canadian record, for after considerable search through weekly newspaper archives, no similar case could be found.

Furthermore, *The Journal* is now the oldest business in Humboldt, all others existing at the time of its birth having disappeared.

The Journal has a somewhat unique connection with provincial history. It was started in 1905 by R. A. and W. B. Telfer, the year that Saskatchewan became a province, and Hon. Walter Scott, the province's first premier was a cousin of Robert A., the grand-daddy of the Telfer newspaper family.

During the 60 years of *The Journal's* existence, the various Telfers had a few experiences of a more or less unusual nature.

In the memory of Walter Paul Telfer (second generation) two appear to be most easily recalled no doubt because of their seriocomic nature.

Once a Nova Scotia cod liver oil company demanded $10,000 for damages it claimed were caused to its reputation by a Humboldt druggist's advertisement in *The Journal*. Robert Adam Telfer replied that the threat did not worry him a bit as he didn't have ten dollars let alone ten thousand. Nothing more was heard of the matter.

Following the death of R. A. Telfer, in 1953, his widow spent a great deal of time in the office. She developed an aversion to a certain rural correspondent, a woman of the aggressive type. One day while her son Walter was out of the office, Mrs. Telfer Sr. had to deal with the correspondent, as usual, hard to get along with. The lady was leaving as Walter returned. Mrs. Telfer glared at the departing lady and said: "I hope she breaks a leg." It seems that the words were barely spoken when it was learned that the correspondent had indeed broken her leg, when she stumbled on a curb a short distance down the street.

At present assisting his father Walter, is Don. L., who was raised amid the atmosphere of family newspaper life, and is well qualified in news and editorial writing.

* * *

Father and son, W. A. and R. S. Reid, published *The Kindersley Clarion* for several years from a newspaper office without a commercial printing department. They turned the latter over to an employee on finding at times that there was some conflict between the two branches of the business.

It would appear than no other weekly newspaper has ever operated in Saskatchewan without a commercial printing department.

The innovation was quite a success, no doubt due to the fact that each business had uninterrupted supervision. The total turnover of each eventually equalled the total revenue of the previously combined businesses.

Poetry was more than a by-product from the pens of both the Reids, with every issue of *The Clarion* containing at least one poem of a timely nature. At a moment's notice, each seemed to be able to dash off a verse or two in a hurry, in response to almost any situation. As often as not, the two poets used as a desk the sloping feedboard of the cylinder newspaper press.

R. S. (Bob) Reid is now editor of *The Union Farmer*, official organ of The National Farmers' Union, and published in Saskatoon.

During the six years that he edited *The Clarion*, he wrote more than 300 weekly rhymes, many of which also appeared in other publications.

He tells of how they always enjoyed showing people the way the newspaper was produced, partly because the break from routine work was often welcome for its own sake.

One lady, at the completion of her tour, exclaimed, "My goodness I never realized there was so much to it. I always thought you just . . ." At this point she paused in frustration as she groped for words to describe her obviously vague understanding of the printing process. Finally she voiced the following inept, but somehow expressive conclusion: ". . . sort of put things in the paper."

* * *

When A. C. Stack took over *The Meadow Lake Progress* in 1933, it was the most northerly Saskatchewan weekly newspaper. He travelled more than 450 miles to attend association conventions in Regina. He had two assistants which he alternated as required between the printing office and the general store which he also owned. It has never been clear whether these two helpers were printers being taught the operation of a general store, or store clerks learning the printing trade.

* * *

Memories of Charlie Hynds, Mark Twain's double, publisher of *The Lumsden News-Record* still linger in his home town. The old office building in which his plant was located, remains empty but still carries the original newspaper office sign, including his name.

* * *

D. J. Hartley had to take back his newspaper *The Kerrobert Citizen* on some five different occasions, through failure of the purchasers to fulfill their contracts. Mrs. Hartley had become so accustomed to this routine, that following her husband's death she felt that there must have been something wrong with the last sale arrangement when the purchaser, on making the final payment on his agreement, demanded title to the property.

* * *

Jim McGowan, publisher of *The Watrous Signal* always appreciated a bit of dry humor. On hearing of the farcical claim of ownership of Mars by a Toronto group, he wrote to them to advise that he was ready to move his plant to that planet at any time they provided transportation. He stipulated only one condition. He must be given a corner lot. He received a reply worded in the finest of legal terms, granting him title to the kind of lot he desired.

John Pinckney, of *The Rosetown Eagle*, is a highly respected citizen, who has filled nearly every public office available in his home town. His newspaper is held in high esteem.

The year he was president of the Canadian Weekly Newspapers Association, M. A. Wilson and E. N. Carter, publishers of *The Wilkie Press*, won first prize in the association's editorial competition. This is a much coveted award so the Saskatchewan Weekly Newspapers Association decided that its significance should be properly publicized. The Wilkie Board of Trade agreed to sponsor a public event as the two local publishers were extremely popular men. Pinckney was slated to do the honors for the CWNA.

In the course of all the eulogizing which followed the banquet, it became quite apparent that Wilson and Carter were familiarly known locally as "Happy" and "Pappy".

When it came time for Pinckney's presentation address, he began by stating he was much impressed by this circumstance. "I haven't yet reached that stage in my publishing career," he said. "Around Rosetown people refer to me as 'that bastard Pinckney.' "

*   *   *

Jack and Joe Ives of Tisdale, Saskatchewan, are the antithesis of old time printers who never stayed long in any one place. Aside from Jack being one and one-half years old when he came with his parents to Tisdale, both have spent all their lives there. They hold a record that is most unusual.

They were raised in Tisdale, educated there, served their apprenticeship in *The Recorder* office, and finally purchased the business and plant in 1953. Indications are they will continue to publish it for many years to come. They like the Tisdale people and the people like them. *The Recorder* is presently one of the top circulation weeklies in Saskatchewan, proving that the two home-town boys have made good.

Jack was president of the Saskatchewan Weekly Press Association, 1966-67.

They recall that at one time their newspaper was named *The Carrot River Valley Recorder*. Oddly enough, another weekly just 25 miles away at Melfort, was called *The Carrot River Valley Journal*, to provide the most cumbersome titles of all Saskatchewan newspapers. This reference to the local area was engendered by the wide publicity given the area at the peak of the inrush of settlers. Both newspapers finally deleted "Carrot River Valley" from their titles.

It is to be regretted that so many unusual experiences of the weekly newspapermen who started business in Saskatchewan just after the turn of the century, were not recorded in any way. Many of them might have become "folk tales", to be passed down from generation to generation within the printing fraternity.

It is therefore something of a delight to discover a story in *The Tisdale Recorder* of September, 1936, of an exigency some 30 years before, and how it was overcome. All in all, it was a feat probably never duplicated anywhere before or since, displaying the versatility of the early printer in critical situations.

When E. W. Schell, in December 1906, unpacked and began to set up his printing plant in Tisdale he found that much of the spacing material he purchased had not been included in the shipment.

Spacing material—"quads," "leads," and "furniture"— is just as necessary as type in making up forms. These items, in varying sizes, fill up the blank areas at the end of and between lines of type as well as filling in the larger open white spaces appearing on all pieces of printed matter. The shortage placed him in a most embarrassing situation.

He had promised the townspeople to have the first issue of his weekly paper in the mails on Dec. 20. Advertisers were greatly enthused. They were proud to have a newspaper start up in their town, especially at a time when their first advertising messages would be in the hands of the public just before Christmas.

How could he honor the promise he had made?

He quickly conceived a temporary solution to his problem.

With jack-knife, saw and sand paper he manufactured, out of wood, with surprising accuracy, enough of the material needed to fill out the newspaper forms. It required many late night and early morning hours to do this, but No. 1 issue went to press on time.

Only a printer, familiar with the need for accuracy in size of all spacing material, can fully appreciate the feat that Schell performed. However, some idea of Schell's achievement might be understood by the layman, when told that even the difference of a thickness of ordinary paper in the size of type space, or quad, or furniture, can give rise to numerous aggravating printing problems after the type forms are put on the press.

*　　*　　*

The town of Rosthern, Saskatchewan, has an unusual newspaper and printing history. It has a population of only 1400. With the exception of the larger cities, no other provincial center has been the home of so many different newspapers printed in other than the English language.

A Ruthenian publication, *New Country*, was first published in 1912. It was short lived.

Die Deutche Press, printed in German, was issued from 1913-1915.

From 1933-1940 the Conference of the Defenceless Mennonite Brethren in Christ in North America published *Evangelisationsbote* as a semi-monthly.

In 1949 *Der Kinderbote*, a magazine for children, began under the direction of the General Conference of Mennonites in North America. Strangely enough, the bulk of its subscribers lived in South America, so it was eventually moved there.

The Immigration Messenger, a weekly—later *Der Bote*, was started in 1924 by Deitrich H. Epp, a high school teacher from Russia. In 1945, a German paper in the United States was absorbed by it, boosting circulation to 7800.

On the death of Epp in 1955, the business was taken over by his foster son, John Heese. When the latter died in 1960, *Der Bote* was acquired by the General Conference of Mennonite Churches in North America, and is now being issued from Saskatoon.

The reason for the centralization of the Mennonite papers in Rosthern was not so much the concentration of that particular group of people in the area, but rather the presence of Mr. Epp, who saw the need for a publication to serve as a bond for the many immigrants who came to Canada in the 1920s and were scattered across the country from Ontario to British Columbia.

The Mennonites were all either of Dutch or German descent. They were the first to settle around Rosthern, coming there as early as 1891 from Alberta, Manitoba and the United States.

At present their majority in the Rosthern area has been cut to about 55 percent of the local population. The Ukrainian faction makes up about 35 per cent. and the remaining 10 percent is composed of Anglo-Saxons, French, German (Lutheran), Scandinavian and a few Metis.

Deitrich H. Epp, on starting *Der Bote* set all the type for it by hand and had the paper printed by a local plant. Later he purchased the press facilities in Rosthern where an English language weekly was already being published and thus obtained a permanent home for his German weekly.

However, the first weekly newspaper to be published in Rosthern was *The Saskatchewan Valley News*, beginning in 1903. This has been the only English language paper to be issued there. After some dozen or more changes in proprietorship, it is now owned by Frank Letkemann who has been successful in building its subscription list into one of the largest among all Saskatchewan weeklies.

*   *   *

Saskatchewan weekly newspapers in their variety of size, location, technical make-up and content can provide many surprises to the uninitiated. One of these may be found at Muenster, six miles east of Humboldt. Muenster's population is rated as being barely 125, yet the local printing plant issues a newspaper with a paid-in-advance subscription list of more than 10,000 in Saskatchewan alone.

The publication is *The Prairie Messenger*, published weekly by the Order of St. Benedict. While its columns carry a selection of news stories of general interest, it does stress articles relating to social and religious themes.

It was the immigration in 1903 of a German colony from Minnesota to settle in the area of which Humboldt is now the center, which brought about the beginning of the *Messenger*.

With the erection of a few buildings, the name "Muenster" was attached to them, and it was there the Benedictine Fathers set up their first monastery in Canada.

Realizing that a Catholic newspaper issued in the German language would be a great unifying force among the immigrants, the Fathers arranged for the publication of the paper with the first issue appearing in February 1904. It was then the only Catholic newspaper in the German language in all of Canada.

It was first printed and mailed from Winnipeg but there were difficulties encountered with the editor 600 miles distant.

Beginning in 1905, a printing plant with the necessary staff had been installed at Muenster.

Legislation passed during the war years compelled the paper to appear in English from October 1918 to December 1919. In the course of time, many of the early pioneers who spoke and read only German, passed away. Subscriptions gradually dwindled, for the younger generation was not conversant with the language of its forefathers. So the original *Prairie Messenger* discontinued publication in 1947.

However, the Benedictines had not lost sight of the importance of the press. As early as 1922 they had founded an English language newspaper, *St. Peter's Messenger.* Later, to indicate the wide field it covered, the name was changed to *The Prairie Messenger,* under which title it still continues.

* * *

Jim C. Adair, now owner of *The Raymond Review (Alberta,)* was one of the generation of young men most affected by the depression years of the 1930s. But all of the harshness of those dismal times failed to affect his good nature and warm personality.

It was at Grandview, Manitoba, where he first began to set type, having been attracted to the business by that stately gentleman, A. G. Graham, who later published *The Canora Courier.*

In 1929, his father was invited to purchase *The Grandview Exponent,* being assured that son Jim knew enough about the trade to operate the business successfully. So at the age of 21 he became editor, printer and manager.

Depression conditions forced his father to close his insurance office and join his son who then had the unique experience of teaching the trade to his father. Jim tries to discount his own printing skill at that time by telling of how he hired a retired 90-year-old printer for $12 a week who could hand-set type faster than he could.

The struggle against depression conditions was a losing one, and lack of business forced the shop to close.

Like so many printers, Jim had become a proficient bandsman, playing several different brass instruments. His enthusiasm in this field led him to recruit a small brass band from among weekly newspapermen right across Canada to play at the Canadian Weekly Newspapers Association convention in Vancouver in 1935, with Andrew King as conductor.

In the summer of 1936 he went on the road with a travelling dance band which earned little better than a starvation income.

Then he went to Flin Flon, Manitoba, where he worked on both newspapers there and played with all the local dance bands.

Finally he revived the Saskatchewan weekly, *The Eatonia Enterprise*, and later moved to Raymond, Alberta.

He has three sons in the trade; recently had a visiting grandson spend some time in the *Enterprise* shop, learning a bit about printing. Said Jim: "He is too young to know better, but seriously, I have enjoyed the weekly newspaper business, and would do it all over again if I had the chance . . . but differently."

* * *

It was in 1908 that Charles Lancaster, a Boer War veteran and a recent immigrant from England, accompanied by his wife and son Reg, arrived in Melfort. He came to set up the business and plant of *The Melfort Journal* for Dr. Shadd, a colored medical doctor who had taken a fancy to owning a newspaper as well as providing opposition to *The Melfort Moon*, a Liberal Supporter.

Times were not too prosperous in those days and the task of producing a weekly newspaper involved working long hours and considerable pressure. All the type used in news columns and advertisements was set by hand. However, some of the strain was lifted when the page forms were finally put on the bed of the newspaper cylinder press. At least it was then possible to escape from some strenuous labor. There were many strong armed Indians around, all attracted by the novelty of the work, who were eager to crank the big flywheel of the press for the double pleasure of seeing the sheets of paper being printed and the cash reward at the end of the run.

In 1911 Charles purchased the business from Dr. Shadd to begin an ownership involving more members of one family than any other weekly in the Canadian west.

Following his death, his four sons, Reg, George, Gordon and Pat, together with his widow, had a hand in the continuing growth of the *Journal.*

A partnership was formed under the name of The *Melfort Journal Publishing Co.* Then when Reg entered the employ of the Canadian Northern Railway his three brothers set up another company named Lancaster Printers Ltd. which contracted to rent building and plant from the publishing company

The first home of the *Journal* still remains a part of a much enlarged structure.

Charles Lancaster left a wonderful heritage through his love of music, particularly choral. During the 1920s, people of Melfort and district were enthralled with his presentations of musical comedies such as Gilbert and Sullivan's *Pinafore, Mikado* and *Pirates of Penzance.* A love of music grew up throughout the community that has continued throughout the years, with a number of manifestations. In 1968 the Melfort Kinsmen School Band of 60 pieces toured England, Scotland and Holland, and was given an enthusiastic reception everywhere it performed.

George, Gord and Pat have displayed a high standard of journalism in their operation of *The Journal.* It has the third largest circulation among all member newspapers of the Saskatchewan Weekly Newspapers Association.

* * *

Several years ago Gordon Juckes, publisher of *The Melville Advance* became associated with the Canadian Amateur Hockey Association and found this closer contact with sport very much to his liking. Later he was appointed executive director of the association and sold his newspaper.

That move put him right in the center of the whirl of problems, fancied and real, presented by managers, players and fans connected with any vigorous and keenly contested game, particularly hockey.

His position is a marked change from the more serene routine of weekly newspaper editing and publishing but Gordon continues to be absorbed by the challenge of sports writers and fans with their varied opinions on such things as Canada's national hockey team and support of pee-wee hockey.

OUR EDITOR'S PRAYER

Lord, grant me patience when the wayward world
Feels not my anxious tug upon the rein.
When words of wisdom from my pen, are hurled
Back in my face, with anger and disdain.

Remind me, Lord, that when my course is run
And Thou from earthly trials has set me free,
My victory for Thy kingdom will be won
If Thou and I have wrought a change in me.

—R. S. REID, in *The Kindersley Clarion*, 1959.

Chapter 24

MOVE TO ESTEVAN

In 1940, when the illness of Donald C. Dunbar, publisher of *The Estevan Mercury*, forced him to give up an active life, he asked me if I would consider purchasing the business.

The suggestion was an attractive one, since *The Rouleau Enterprise* as a newspaper was no longer showing a profit. Due to Rouleau's close proximity to Regina, with its retail stores with large stocks of goods, sale prices and enticing shopping surroundings, was draining off from Rouleau an ever-increasing volume of business.

Local retail establishments in the town continued to disappear, one after the other.

Its main street, which thirty years before, had been packed from end to end with stores providing every need, was down to six retail establishments. The turnover of each was but a fraction of that of earlier years.

The backbone of newspaper support was gone, just as had happened in dozens of other towns in the province.

My two sons, Stirling and William, were associated with me and had decided that newspaper work and printing would be their lifetime calling.

Estevan at that time had a population of 2500. It was the trading center of a large area, coupled with natural resources giving promise of industrial expansion. Locations with such advantages were rare indeed in the rural west, which was beginning to suffer from the impact of the mechanical age and economic change.

I went to Estevan to appraise the situation and ascertain

183

the price set by Mr. Dunbar on his property, plant and business.

He was too ill to be interviewed, but his son, Donald M., gave me all the information I desired. It was decided that I would return in a week's time to complete the purchase.

But the latter was not to be. The day before I was to return to Estevan, Donald phoned to say: "Put off your trip for a couple of weeks, Andy. Dad died this afternoon."

Later, he called again to advise that a family huddle had decided he himself should carry on the business, even though it meant resigning his position with the International Nickel Co. of Sudbury, Ontario, as editor of the INCO Triangle and head of employer-employee relations department of that company.

Following the death of his mother late in 1943, Donald M. contacted me to see if I would again consider buying *The Mercury*. The INCO people were anxious to have him back on their staff and it was a position offering a fine salary.

He came to Rouleau to see me. It did not take us more than half an hour to agree on price and terms with a take-over scheduled for Feb. 1, 1944. I immediately began to prepare for the move.

J. E. Willoughby of *The Milestone Mail* agreed to continue publication of *The Enterprise* from Milestone. I sold my house and wound up some business odds and ends.

On January 30th, I took the train to Estevan and was greeted by Don with a hearty handshake. I booked accommodation at a hotel. The balance of the afternoon and the evening, with a fine dinner served by Mrs. Dunbar, was a social period of chit-chat and reminiscence unbroken by even a hint of the purpose of my arrival in town.

The next morning, Don informed me that his lawyer was out of town and would not be back for three or four days, so the required legal papers would not be ready for signature until he prepared them on his return.

"But," he said, "You just take over tomorrow, February 1st, the day we agreed you would take possession."

I did. I collected a few subscriptions, began to look for news, chased after advertising copy, priced a couple of job work orders and discovered that Estevan people, were most kind and courteous. and the casual way I took over the business did not strike me until several days later when the lawyer entered the scene with numerous ponderous documents to sign.

From the viewpoint of anyone in the legal profession, the preliminaries leading up to my acquisition of *The Mercury* could only be labelled as just childish. Neither Don nor I had even made a single notation on paper as to any of the conditions of purchase upon which we had verbally agreed.

What a remarkable example it was of mutual confidence in the reliability of each other's spoken words.

The shop staff at the time consisted of three men and a part time bindery girl.

My son Stirling was overseas in the Canadian forces. William had remained at Rouleau to operate the show print business until the summer rush was over and until an addition to the *Mercury* building could be built, to accommodate the poster plant. The size of the addition was more than double that of the original building.

Our new location provided the opportunity to drop the somewhat commonplace name of *Enterprise Show Print* and replace it with the more distinctive title of *King Show Print.*

The moving of the poster plant from Rouleau was a simple procedure compared with the work and time required to dismantle and re-erect machinery in earlier years.

The big poster press was simply jacked up, underlaid with rollers and winched onto a transport truck. It was in Estevan in a few hours. In fact if urgency had dictated, it could have been connected with power and running before the day had passed. When I first bought it at Rouleau, a machinist took six days to assemble the dismantled parts shipped in crates and boxes, the only way in which large machines could be transported in those days.

In a sense, the taking over of *The Mercury* presented a real challenge. How could I hope to sustain its reputation following such a brilliant news writer as Donald M., as well as the editorial excellence of his father Donald C. Dunbar?

Donald Culloden Dunbar, editor and publisher of *The Estevan Mercury* for 33 years until his death in 1940, was one

185

of the most widely known western newspaper writers in his generation. In his later years he became known as the dean of journalism in the prairie west.

His was a colorful personality. He often appeared at conventions in attire usually associated with some other professions in the early days. There was an aura of dignity about him which was accentuated by his frock coat, and as years passed and his heavy thatch of hair became almost pure white, he became a striking figure in spite of his small stature.

For several years the newspaper featured his own editorials. Each week he wrote seven columns of bright and scholarly copy, dealing with local and national events and expressing opinion carrying influence well beyond the local sphere. This was in addition to assuming many other time-consuming duties in the conduct of his business.

He found that most readers, on receiving their copy of *The Mercury* would glance at the headlines on the front page and then turn to the inside editorial page "to see what Donald had to say this week."

He had a way with words. His use of adjectives was particularly adroit; he was capable of withering sarcasm on occasion. There was no mistaking his opinions and conclusions on any subject he chose to deal with, even though at times he made enemies thereby. In this regard he believed in the power of the press being used to fight all forms of evil—social, economic and political.

On one occasion he was sued for libel by a local citizen. the latter won a moral victory by being awarded damages in the amount of one dollar with plaintiff and defendant each to pay their own legal costs.

Donald commented on this in something like these words: "Seems the complainant caught me with just the tip of my toe over the line."

At one time he declared that "conventions and service clubs are a God-send for the four-flusher." That was in the days when organizations for mutual benefit were misunderstood. Some were then just in the process of selling themselves to the public and those people who were, or should have been, most particularly concerned.

The sequel to this sweeping declaration came later. He eventually proved the inaccuracy of his own statement. He finally became president of the Saskatchewan Division of the Canadian Weekly Newspapers Association. He served in that office with considerable distinction.

Once a group of irate coal miners, irritated to violence by an opinion he had expressed, came to wreck his plant. Hearing of the threat he hurried to the scene and in front of his office finally got them to listen to him. So cleverly did he address them that it was not long until they all walked quietly away.

On another occasion he added a western touch to an incident in which he innocently became involved. It happened during First World War when a group of intensely loyal citizens became enraged at a remark made by a certain businessman.

Conscription had just been introduced and under the regulations, Germans were exempt. The remark made was to the effect that "the government considered one German better than one hundred conscripts."

One day members of the vigilance committee happened to gather on the main street at the same time as their target was seen walking around a corner to a cross street. The group took after him, and the hunted man began to run and dodged into the first open door which happened to be that of *The Mercury* office. As he ran into the back shop, he shouted to Dunbar that the crowd was going to lynch him.

Dunbar quickly saw what could happen to his plant if the mob ever got into the building in pursuit of their victim. He suddenly remembered that an old revolver was in the drawer of his desk. Snatching it out he hurried to the door in time to meet the front runners of the mob.

Pointing the weapon, he shouted so that all could hear, in a voice that rang with warning and sincerity: "Everybody stand back, or I will shoot."

It had the desired result. The chase was abandoned. The gun did not even contain as much as a blank cartridge, but Donald had handled the situation in true western movie tradition.

Over the years, Dunbar moved *The Mercury* office to

several different locations, leading him to refer to his newspaper as "the peregrinating weekly."

During one move, the newspaper press was only half way between locations on publication day so he printed that week's issue in the middle of the street. The press was driven by a stationary gasoline engine and the sheets of paper were fed into the press by hand. Many people saw for the first time how a newspaper was printed. People kept talking about it for days on end.

It was a most regrettable thing that a fire which destroyed his plant in 1925, also destroyed *Mercury* files up to that date. His finest work went up in smoke. Some of his articles were journalistic gems, ranking easily with the works of some of the leading journalists of this continent. But with advancing years he began to lose the fire shown in his previous writings; yet he still retained a prominent position among weekly newspaper editors. When he had written his final "30," journalism in the Canadian west lost its most colorful char-acter of the decade.

No one since has quite filled the niche created by Donald Culloden Dunbar.

With the return of my son Stirling, at the close of the Second World War, the partnership of King and Sons was set up. Stirling took over management of *The Mercury* and the news desk. William shouldered the responsibilities con-nected with the poster and commercial printing department, including that of contact man with fair and exhibition ex-ecutives.

An additional linotype was purchased, and automatic presses installed together with other modern equipment. The staff was constantly growing in numbers so that by the late '50s between 30 and 35 were on the payroll, to make it the largest among all Estevan town industrial establishments.

The heavy seasonal volume of circus and carnival printing had then been augmented by an increased amount of commercial printing which was partially spurred by the expansion of the adjacent oil fields.

The Mercury did not lag. Its weekly average number of pages increased, and the subscription list reached a figure that at the time was only exceeded by two or three other weeklies in the whole province. That figure was very close to 4400 paid-in-advance and guaranteed by the Audit Bureau of Circulations.

Another addition was made to the building which more than tripled its original size. It was built with foundations ready to take on the weight of a second storey, to take care of expansion in the future. But unexpected things can happen to everyone.

One morning there was a 'phone call from Calgary. It was made by the president of *The Daily Echo* of Liverpool, England. After the first formal greeting, he said: "I understand your business is for sale."

This was news to us. The only reply I could muster on such short notice was, "yes, everyone has his price."

Negotiations began by letter and cable and finally on January 1, 1958, *The Estevan Mercury* and King Show Print became the property of the Liverpool company, operated under the name of The Estevan Mercury Limited. Stirling was named vice-president of the company and manager, with William, a director in charge of the show print and commercial printing department. I remained as editorial writer. The work was not difficult to carry on, even though my wife and I spent five winter months away from Estevan each year. Over the years, we visited in over 45 states, wandering here and there and gathering material for stories and articles for a small string of daily and weekly newspapers and other publications. San Benito, Texas became our southern home.

It would not be truthful to state that I had no regrets over the sale of *The Mercury* and King Show Print. To relinquish any business in which a keen interest, effort and hard work have been invested is something that is not easily done without some feeling of loss.

Of all types of business it would seem that the most difficult one to part with is that of a newspaper. There is a sentimentality about it all that cannot be ignored.

No other business enmeshes its staff and management as does a newspaper. No other business is so intimately personalized.

A newspaper—and particularly a weekly newspaper—is the final and visible concentration of individual thought, study, planning and technical art, centered around the assembled news of the community, together with its atmosphere, the whole transferred from mind to paper to create a personality of its own by mirroring the talent and the skill of all those involved in its production. And that is what makes a newspaper so different from the mechanically produced merchandise which fill the shelves of retail stores.

You know, it's kinda nice at that, to be able to walk downtown (any hometown) and meet a dozen folks who think nothing of calling your grandfather a horse thief, and smiling in the process.

—JIM GREENBLAT, *Swift Current Sun.*

Chapter 25

PERSONALITIES

WALTER ASHFIELD

W alter Ashfield, for many years publisher of *The Grenfell Sun*, was born with all the instincts of a military man. This was reflected not only in his enviable record during active service in both First and Second World Wars, but also in the precise manner in which he conducted his business affairs.

In the latter instance a routine after the pattern of military discipline prevailed in the operation of his office and printing plant, unless totally uncontrollable circumstances intervened.

He insisted that the plant's machinery be running at 8 a.m. and that it close down at supper time unless overtime was absolutely necessary—a situation that rarely developed.

He maintained that a full day's work without any loitering would produce all the regular run of necessary work; too much night work was a disease which sapped the staff's strength for day work.

Yet he was far from being a harsh employer. He simply set reasonable rules which he insisted must be observed and in doing so gained the respect of his staff. He disciplined himself with a routine which resulted in an even flow of material and instructions from the front office to the back shop.

The depth of thought in his weekly column "Along the Line With Ash," was not recognized by everyone. It was actually a bit of a "double entendre." It contained news and comment dealing with Canadian Pacific Railway main line centers, but was also written right along the lines of clear thinking and persuasive suggestion, with no punches pulled.

There was also a First World War connotation to the

title, as well—the contrast of busy things and dull things happening from day to day along the front line trenches. Walter never explained this—his manner of thinking—but appeared to hope that his readers would just pick it up.

He was seriously wounded in France during the First World War and purchased *The Grenfell Sun* following his discharge in 1918. For a time he was still somewhat handicapped physically, but he quickly built up the newspaper into one of the sturdiest Saskatchewan weeklies in its circulation class.

No matter what anyone may have called it—habit or determination—it was that inbred military discipline which caused him to continue writing editorials and his weekly column while a patient in the Department of Veterans Affairs Wing of Regina General Hospital. At that time, he was unable to sit up but had either to lie down or stand. He did his writing by the laborious and painful expedient of standing in front of a typewriter placed on a high table and typing out his copy.

When his affliction became malignant, he underwent the then new betatron treatments in Saskatoon. These were most unpleasant and disturbing, yet he interviewed specialists who operated the equipment, and wrote a series of articles on the treatment in the hope that it might be of some interest and benefit to other cancer victims.

When the Second World War broke out in 1939 and his eldest son Cliff went overseas, he pleaded with military authorities to have his fitness category raised so that he, too, might go overseas on active service.

His plea was pushed aside but he was authorized to raise the 65th Battery, Royal Canadian Artillery. One of the great disappointments of his life came when this unit was sent to the battlefront, while he was retained in Canada in a training role.

In the years which followed he built a fine reputation as major of the 22nd Brigade at Dundurn, Saskatchewan, and later became second-in-command of the 12th District Depot at Regina, and finally commanding officer of the 22nd Field Regiment, Royal Canadian Artillery.

Finally, the day came when he had the pleasure and

privilege of turning the latter command over to his son Cliff, the first command of a Canadian unit ever to pass in direct succession from father to son.

He was not lacking in appreciation of wry humor, and this was evident at most unexpected times. For example, a new addition was being made to the Wolseley Hospital in which he was a patient for a short time previous to his death. One day a nurse ushered a workman into his private ward and told him that the man had come to take some measurements.

He looked up, smiled, and said, "What for? My coffin?"

However, it was not a manifestation of humor which he displayed on another occasion when, on leaving a theatre following a matinee and blinded by the direct rays of the sun, he crashed his 215 pounds through the plate glass exterior door. He sought out the manager and tore a military strip off the latter for his carelessness in tolerating such a booby trap.

The important posts which Walter Ashfield held in both national and provincial newspapers associations indicates the status he held among weekly publishers. He was president of the Saskatchewan Division, CWNA, in 1930-31, and president of the Canadian Weekly Newspapers Association, 1946-47.

He succeeded Sam Dornan as secretary-manager of the Saskatchewan Division in 1947 and filled that position until illness in 1952 forced him to resign.

The association records he kept during those five years were painstaking in detail, clarity and neatness. He was an admirable successor to Sam Dornan, in that he competently maintained the long-standing pleasant relationships with government people during a somewhat disturbed period of political history in Saskatchewan.

SOLOMON M. BONNEAU, LL.B., Q.C.

The life story of Solomon M. Bonneau of Gravelbourg, Saskatchewan, is a fascinating one.

Born in 1888, the charm of his personality is as fresh and irresistible as ever. He has achieved notable success, not only within his chosen profession, but in the inspiration to others, through his outstanding community leadership.

Among all the weekly newspaper publishers in Saskatchewan he holds a unique distinction. His *L'Etoile de Gravelbourg* was the only bilingual (French-English) news weekly to be published in the province.

He founded, edited and published more than a bakers' dozen of other newspapers serving an equal number of south Saskatchewan towns and added to higher over-all standards of the weekly press through editorials of high journalistic excellence.

Solomon Bonneau practiced law with meticulous care. When he closed down his law practice a few years ago, the Law Society of Saskatchewan gave him well-deserved recognition by presenting him with a senior life membership certificate in the Association.

He served in many public offices in his immediate community. There was hardly a single organization in Gravelbourg that he did not serve as president. Provincially, he was actively associated with other groups through their highest offices.

He was mayor of Gravelbourg for seven terms, and chairman and trustee of the Gravelbourg School Board for 25 years.

He still found time to serve with the rank of pilot officer in Royal Canadian Air Force during the Second World War.

It is little wonder he earned the title of "Monsieur Gravelbourg."

Mr. Bonneau was born south of Winnipeg, where his father operated a farm. In his youth he did not fail to use and develop his mental and physical assets. Money was not too plentiful—a common state of those days—so during his university days he made good use of his bilingualism, a bicycle and an ability to report news events clearly, correctly and with a bit of flair that readers enjoyed.

He became a reporter for *The Winnipeg Daily Telegram* in the hours he could spare each day from his studies. His bicycle would take him to a point of interest faster than any street car. Results were gratifying, since he managed to beat the inflexible press deadline on many occasions.

After graduating from Manitoba Law School, his journalistic ability won him the editorship of *The Northwest Review,* a weekly newspaper published in Winnipeg.

He arrived in Gravelbourg in 1918 to relieve a lawyer friend who was going on his honeymoon. Though there were nine lawyers in the town at that time, Solomon engaged in practice with his friend on his return.

It was not long until *L'Etoile de Gravelbourg,* published by C. J. Coulombe, stirred his newspapering blood and he began writing for it in his spare time.

When Mr. Bonneau took over that paper in 1926, it was published in both English and French, and was the only bilingual newspaper in Saskatchewan. Its page makeup as far as conditions would permit consisted of two columns of news in English, two columns in French, separated by two columns filled with advertising. This arrangement was adopted to protect national advertising, such as liquor and industrial products, which was in English.

As time passed, the English section proved more profitable and gradually took preference, and this led to two separate newspapers, which became the parents of a chain of 19 weeklies serving smaller towns throughout a comparatively wide area.

Mr. Bonneau tells how during the depression years, little cash was obtained from the practice of law, but through the group of newspapers he was able to swap subscriptions and advertising space for farm produce and other household and personal needs, so he and his family weathered the "dirty '30s" in quite a satisfactory manner without going on relief.

A little later, with prosperity returning to the prairies, he found his law practice making greater demands on his time. He then began to turn the newspaper responsibilities over to his son Paul, who by 1961 was in complete charge in addition to carrying on a thriving real estate business.

Though at that time Mr. Bonneau retired from active participation in newspaper work locally, he still could not subdue completely the fascination which news writing held for him, and still continues to file dispatches for various daily newspapers in Saskatchewan.

PHIL FLUDE

There is no doubt, had he so desired, Phil Flude of Indian Head, Saskatchewan, could have become a noted columnist in the metropolitan newspaper field, Canadian or broader in scope.

It was his contentment with the homey atmosphere of his home town, still enriched with the culture of the pioneers, and the degree of satisfaction he obtained in carrying on his own business, which made him brush aside any temptation to move into the stress of city life, where richer monetary compensation does not always offset its disadvantages.

Phil is a modest man, sound in judgement, quiet in demeanour but with the sensitivity of a keen student of human nature. Yet he is an activist in a real sense, as shown by his contributions through personal service and leadership in projects for community betterment.

In 1958, the Canadian Broadcasting Corporation recognized his literary talent. He is now providing the CBC with a series of short stories of warm human interest.

But it is as a columnist that he excels. In his own "Casual Glances" which appeared regularly in his newspaper, *The Indian Head News*, he presents entertaining essays and observations that are full of tongue-in-cheek subtleties and comments to stir the intellect, tied in with current events whose effect on future life on this planet are viewed in prophecy for half a century hence.

It was in 1917 that Phil Flude entered the plant of *The Indian Head News* as an apprentice. He was its editor ten years later. By 1950 he was its owner.

The background of *The News* is unusually colorful, not only because of its association with the anxieties of the early settlers just previous to rebellion year of 1885, but with the flow of military and supplies through Fort Qu'Appelle occasioned by the uprising. At that time *The News* was published at this important military post, under the title of *The Qu'Appelle Vidette*.

Army volunteers were trained at the Fort in anticipation of a native uprising.

The plant and business was moved to Indian Head in 1897, carrying the name, *The Vidette*, with it. J. D. McAra became editor and he was followed later by his brother James. Some years later both became prominent in the real estate business in Regina.

The Vidette was the fourth weekly to be started in the area served by the main line of the C.P.R., being preceded by *The Regina Leader* on March 1, 1883, *The Moose Jaw News* in April 1883 and *The Moosomin Courier* on Oct. 2, 1884. The first issue of *The Vidette* at Fort Qu'Appelle was dated Oct. 9, 1884.

Beginning in 1885 a weekly newspaper under the name of *The Progress*, had been started at Qu'Appelle, which at that time was named Troy.

In 1898 this newspaper began to publish a portion of its issue under the name of *The Fort Qu'Appelle Vedette*, no doubt hoping that the altered spelling of the name would enable it to use the similarly pronounced word to its advantage.

Such hope was quickly snuffed out. J. D. McAra immediately took legal action and *The Progress* at once altered the name in question to *The Valley Echo*.

It was in 1912 that John Miller changed the name of *The Indian Head Vidette* to *The Indian Head News*.

Phil Flude likes to tell of how he first learned the meaning of the word "vidette". He realized it was of foreign origin, but had never troubled to trace its source, which is in the Italian language.

During the Second World War he was placed in charge of a Royal Canadian Artillery unit in Europe. The first day a sergeant approached him, saluted and asked it he wished "videttes" to be posted.

Not wishing to display ignorance he told the sergeant to carry on the usual routine. The posting of the sentinels, or pickets, that evening provided him with the meaning of the word.

After serving on the continent, he was invalided home with the rank of major, for a post in the Department of Personnel Selection at London, Ontario, and Regina, Saskatchewan.

A recognition of Phil Flude's talent is not complete without a reprint of one of his "Casual Glance" columns. The one

chosen deals with the appearance of Monsigneur J. Athol
Murray, of Notre Dame College, Wilcox, Saskatchewan, on
a CBC television panel show, under the title "With Ears
Attuned".

Here it is:

"The old man sat before the panel and heard them out.

"They wanted to know his views on whether murder was
ever justified.

"The question was heavily loaded. So were the ones to
follow.

"The querulous young men wanted negatives or affirma-
tives, and very little else.

"When you are a university student, quite a bit of the
world is either black or white. You have to stand up and be
counted. They sharpen one another's wits on just such posers
as this.

"Would Father Murray say it would have been a cardinal
sin to have murdered, for example, Hitler?

"After all, he had murdered by proxy a great number of
million persons, and if someone had bumped him off, look at
the millions who would have been saved.

"They craned forward eagerly, expectant. They had him.

"But they didn't.

"He answered them, using today's contentions, and conventions, plus a little dogma and creed, refusing to be cornered
but giving them answers of the university corridor, or class-
room, or beerfest.

"This they could understand and, so, he answered them
according to their kind. It was conventional replies like this
they sought.

"But he knew a great deal more than this.

"He knew, for example, that you cannot, or could not,
murder Hitler.

"For as an archtype, he represented a furious spirit
abroad in the land, flinging a gigantic shadow across the
world. He was the embodiment of a nation lusting for power
and glory and world fulfillment. Nothing could stand in the
way of such raw triumph, in which one man's life and aims

were supported by the conquering frenzy of a mighty nation's power.

"Kill Hitler, and a hundred—a thousand—would spring into his place. The very essence of Hitler could never be killed.

"And so, knew the embattled priest, the question was hardly even rhetorical.

"It was in his mind that forceful disposing of Hitler's life would have been against divine law and nothing would have been gained. He had an idea that God knew this too. Yes, and doubtless a great deal more.

"He eyed his hearers and the old man's lips moved and twitched. The audience believe he is the victim of a nervous tic, or that the teeth are not quite right. But it is not so. He is holding converse. And with whom?

"Look! There! In the shadows just off the stage! An awesome spectre, luminous shade, one of the Heavenly Host, benignant.

"The admonitory finger points, communion has begun and the old priest hears the message:

" 'Their minds are young, Athol, do not overburden them. Your ears are finely attuned, when you are an old priest, and you see and hear what others do not.'

"The august counsel concludes. The shade is gone.

"Father Murray continues 'under attack.'

"It is difficult to make it clear to young minds, however alert, in the time allotted.

"A 'yes' or 'no' does not clarify the issue, nor does it make clear the belief of the one on pillory.

"They badgered him and baited him, not without good humor, but the barbs were naked, for the program is for just such purpose. He took it all good-naturedly, for when you have reached the pinnacle of Murray's maturity nothing is exactly new to you and you have heard it all before.

"The answers are not easy, nor simple. Neither are they crystal clear unless, like Father Murray, you have lived a lot, listened a lot, and reflected in lifelong meditation.

"He knew so much more than his simple answers indicated.

"His hearers knew a great deal, too.

"But understood a great deal less."

JAMES GREENBLAT

The life history of Jim Greenblat, who for half a century made Swift Current, Saskatchewan, his home, is a fascinating series of experiences not ordinarily encountered in the life of the average journalist.

As soldier, reporter, weekly and daily newspaper editor, propagandist, wartime columnist, public relations officer, promoter and sports enthusiast, he filled all these assignments with marked distinction.

It is very doubtful if any other Canadian weekly news-paperman was ever called upon to participate in so many different roles.

He was born at Winkler, Manitoba, in 1895. His father was a Russian Jewish immigrant and one of the first mer-chants in the town that was the center of the first area of Mennonite colonies in Canada.

He was educated at Winkler, Winnipeg and Swift Current, graduating from the latter's high school in 1913. He then articled with a Swift Current law firm.

His enlistment in the army, while under age, shortly after the outbreak of the First World War, indicated the spirit that was his. He had already grasped the meaning of personal freedom in a peaceful land as compared to subjection under an outright monarchial old world military regime.

His false statement of age was discovered. He was taken out of the army but that did not deter him from re-enlisting in 1915 with the 128th battalion.

Wounded at Lens, he returned to action after discharge from hospital and served in France and Belgium until demobil-sation in 1919.

One of the most unusual tasks for which he was chosen during his overseas service was a propaganda tour in Ireland in 1917 during the Sinn Fein trouble. He became one of a group of Canadian Army Staff Instructors along with Irish Canadian Rangers of Montreal, to apply their persuasive powers on the recalcitrant Celts.

Jim felt that sending a Jewish boy along with Irish soldiers from the French province of Quebec to melt down the convictions of the Irish regarding their English neighbors across the Irish Sea, was not the best of political strategy.

Still, a former mayor of Dublin was a Jew.

On arrival at a Dublin dock the group was booed.

One night, three of them got lost in that city and on asking a couple of Irishmen for directions, were told, "go to hell and find your own way." To avoid a riot, the boys in uniform said nothing more but moved out of the area rather quickly.

Six of the principal cities in Ireland were visited and influential citizens interviewed but the propaganda effort was a failure.

Back home in Swift Current after demobilization, Jim again took up the study of law. He found it to be a profession that appeared to offer little latitude for individual expression. His wartime experience had materially changed his hopes and ambitions for the years which lay ahead.

Yet the suddenness with which an opportunity was presented to him in 1923 and started him towards an editor's chair was certainly a rare experience. It came about as a result of Jim writing some sports stuff for *The Swift Current Herald*. The copy had a professional touch which had been quickly noted.

One day, A. S. Bennett, then *The Herald* editor met Jim on the street, stopped and said, "Jim, I'm going east. Would you like to be editor of *The Herald*?"

Would he? It only took Jim a second to accept, and he immediately entered the career for which his personality and talents turned out to be particularly well suited.

In the early 1930s, he transferred to *The Swift Current Sun* under Sam P. Moore and only seven years later, he, Mahlon Hutchison and Robert Moore purchased *The Sun* from the latter's father.

During the Second World War, Jim was chosen by the Wartime Prices and Trade Board to go to Ottawa and write a series of articles to be issued to the weekly press of Canada.

These were for the purpose of clarifying for the public at large, the rulings of the Board. In this work Jim's study of law was a plus factor, enabling him to clearly and concisely present the reasons for restrictions and controls which wartime conditions made necessary. He made readable the usual complex and difficult terminology and language of bureaucracy.

After completing this stint, he was again called back to Ottawa to write a weekly column "Canadiana", for the Wartime Information Board. The columns dealt with the nation's wartime efforts—a propaganda series which did much to maintain national morale. Again it was a case of interpreting bureaucratic language for public understanding.

It was while writing this column that Jim became a target for a front page editorial in *Le Devoir* of Montreal, which objected to a man named Greenblat, from the prairies, sending out an English column to the French weeklies. As a result, a French writer then took over the issuing of a similar French language column for the WIB.

After the war was over and he was again permanently settled in Swift Current, Jim continued for some time to produce a Canadiana column that was published by many weeklies across Canada.

The status that Jim held in weekly newspaperdom is demonstrated by the large number of prizes for editorial and general excellence won by *The Sun* during the years he was associated with it.

During a 12-year stretch from 1939 on, it won the Dominion Textile trophy eight times, for the best editorial page. This cup was for competition in the top classification for weekly newspapers.

Like most weekly newspapermen, Jim was always active in community affairs. He coached one of the best hockey teams Swift Current ever produced. He was secretary of Elmwood Golf Club for many years and for 32 years was either secretary or a director of the Swift Current Chamber of Commerce. It was in this position he was extremely successful in aiding the promotion of Swift Current Frontier Days, a rodeo second only in the west to Calgary Stampede.

He was president of the Swift Current Rotary Club and president of Saskatchewan Division, Canadian Weekly Newspapers Association in 1938 and 1939. In 1958 he was awarded an honorary life membership by that division.

In 1957 he sold his interest in *The Sun* to Bob Moore and Dave Belbeck, but finding retirement a bit boring after the active life he enjoyed, he became public relations officer for Pioneer Co-operative Association, Swift Current, until 1960 when he moved to Saskatoon where he had a son practicing optometry.

The same year he joined the staff of *The Saskatoon Star-Phoenix* as an editorial writer. In 1964, family health dictated a move to the west coast.

Jim Greenblat loved every moment of his career as a newspaperman. "It's been a wonderful life" he once said. "And the old-time newspapermen were great!"

HERBERT THOMAS HALLIWELL

Recalling the pioneering experiences of weekly newspaper publishers in Saskatchewan during the first short decade of this century, serves to provide, in part at least, an understanding of conditions prevailing at that time.

Historians have spent much time and effort in recording the ever-changing impress of political pattern. Other writers at times chronicled in somewhat general terms the then-prevailing economic and social conditions.

Yet very much neglected are the day-by-day events involving individuals which often reflect quite vividly the tenor of the times.

Some of the incidents in which these newsmen participated or observed may seem insignificant and inconsequential in the light of present day standards, but each became a brush stroke altering the perspective of the large composite picture portraying the strivings, ambitions, influences, realities, reactions, skills, joys and sorrows of those years.

One whose brush has added bits of bright color to this historic picture is Herbert Thomas Halliwell.

After learning the printing trade in London, England, and serving with the British Forces in the South African War, he succumbed to the wiles of Canadian immigration agents with their offers of free blocks of prairie land and the wonderful, independent life and profitable occupation of farming.

He could hardly have been less fitted for this environment. He was born and bred a city boy. He was going to a new country where nearly everything was in stark contrast to all he had learned and seen, but he was determined to use all his intellect and brawn to achieving success.

On arriving in Canada, he engaged with a farmer near Oxbow, Saskatchewan, to begin his apprenticeship in agriculture. All the simple farm implements of those days and their manner of use had to be explained to him. No doubt he made many mistakes in operating them.

And then the horses! They appeared to be the most gigantic he had ever seen, and the reluctance with which they responded to his commands made him wonder if they did not have him sized up much better than he understood them.

Plowing long, single furrows in fields was a tiring task and so unrewarding in the perspective of mile upon mile of prairie land lying in loneliness in every direction. The monotony of the job and living in a sod shack clinched the decision that took Tom back to his first love—printing.

His first permanent job was with *The Arcola Star*, owned by A. D. McLeod. For the first year he was paid $12 per week. McLeod was one of a fair number of school teachers who ventured into the newspaper business, having concluded that if as one could write in good style, a good income would be assured.

McLeod was a good citizen but not a printer. He could not set a line of type or feed a Gordon press, but once a week he became a back-shop man. His muscles provided sufficient power to run the press for an hour or so, printing the weekly issue.

Tom Halliwell had been trained as a job, or commercial, printer in England. At Arcola he had to become acquainted with techniques peculiar to the production of newspapers, North American style.

British newspapers at that time were rather insipid looking sheets. Their front pages were almost totally filled with classified advertisements lacking in eye appeal. "Display" ads would often be a group of words such as "Lipton's Tea is Good Tea" or "Use Pears' Soap" set in type not larger than pica (6 lines to one inch depth) and repeated over and over again until the space was filled. A price was never quoted at any time.

The style of composition for advertisements then being developed in the United States had begun to creep into Canada —that of using large type for display headings followed by detailed descriptions of goods offered.

Tom soon familiarized himself with this technique, began to write advertisements for customers and then took on a bit of reporting. He was on his way up.

In 1905, he stepped out for himself and started a newspaper at Manor, Saskatchewan. He printed it on a Washington hand operated press. A son of the local blacksmith came in on publication day to handle the big roller which inked the type forms. Tom began to notice that always at a certain spot on the forms the boy would give the roller a couple of extra strokes and on being asked why he did it, he replied: "That's where my old man's advertisement is."

During Saskatchewan's first election campaign in 1905, Mr. Frederick W. G. Haultain (later Sir Frederick) made an unexpected visit to Manor—unexpected and unannounced because there were no telephones in those days, railway mail service was limited, and country travel was by horse and buggy.

The local Conservatives hastily organized a meeting, and in the evening a dinner was held in the hotel with the party continuing into the early hours of next morning. In the phrase of today, a good time was had by all, even though the political situation in the new province was the main topic of discussion. The well-written, lengthy report of Haultain's visit showed that one newspaperman had found time to relax a while from his busy life and at the same time decide on his political affiliation.

Some years later Tom acquired *The Fort Macleod Gazette* which he published for 21 years.

He was a kindly man, yet so outspoken on his views of many topics that some were inclined to believe he displayed a streak of vindictiveness in his editorial columns. He simply took the position that clear cut expression of opinion was the responsibility of every editor, and in this regard he left his mark throughout the years. And had he equal respect for emphatically expressed opinions of others.

In 1935 the Alberta Weekly Newspapers Association chose him as its president. That was the year the Social Credit party came into power in that province.

It was quite typical of Halliwell to write an open letter addressed to Premier William Aberhart suggesting he either put up or shut up by refraining from "continued claims of misrepresentation by the press, or take action against those newspapers you claim are telling lies." Nothing further was heard of the challenge.

Additional recognition came to Halliwell in 1939 when the Canadian Weekly Newspapers Association elected him its president.

He died September, 1970, at his home in Fort Macleod,

PATRICK GAMMIE LAURIE

Weekly newspapermen of western Canada are proud of the prestige and eminence brought to their profession by Patrick Gammie Laurie, who established *The Saskatchewan Herald* at Battleford; it was the first newspaper in the lonely reaches of the North West Territories.

This indeed was a notable venture, and the man who launched it showed courage, determination, and integrity throughout his career.

His was an intellect shaped in the main by the stresses of a new land and a continuing search for practical solutions to the continuing problems of individuals and governments.

It required courage and vision to purchase in Winnipeg, Manitoba, a meagre lot of printing equipment, load it on an ox cart and head westward for a little hamlet reached only by a few rutted prairie trails. The nearest railroad was then many miles distant, and mail reached Battleford only once every three weeks.

It took Laurie 72 days to make the journey from Winnipeg

with his heavily laden cart, through sunshine and rain, over hills, through valleys, across mudholes, brushland and grass-land.

He had been quick to realize that, with Battleford desig-nated as the new Territorial capital, government printing contracts could most likely be had by a resident printer.

The first issue of *The Saskatchewan Herald* was published on August 25, 1878. Its subscribers required a news service of more than local coverage. Their isolation created an eager-ness for news of faraway places.

Fortunately there was a telegraph line to Edmonton and one to Winnipeg. While the service was irregular, storms would break the lines in isolated stretches, they did bring in enough news dispatches to enable a paper to be issued every two weeks.

Laurie was his own reporter, editor, compositor, pressman, and bookbinder, so he was able to carry on his business as he pleased.

Local advertising was meagre. He was constantly solici-ting advertising from Winnipeg, of products needed in the Battleford area. At no time did he have a substantial income even though newspaper revenues were added to by selling books and seeds on commission, and acting as agent for federal and territorial governments as crown timber agent, issuer of marriage and billiard table licenses, game guardian, coroner, inspector of schools and supervisor of public works. None of these brought him much income. As school inspector, he received $25 per year. He felt he was filling pressing public needs by serving in these many capacities.

He had only four or five years of schooling, yet his edi-torials were of exceptionally high standard, his talent in this regard no doubt being enriched by constant reading and study.

At all times he promoted the welfare of the North West, having great confidence in its future.

It was a sad blow to him (yet accepted without com-plaint) to have the territorial capital moved to Regina in 1883. He died in 1903. His son R. C. Laurie carried on publi-cation of *The Herald* until 1938.

While emphasis has always been placed on Patrick Gammie Laurie's "first" in territorial newspaperdom, his career before he entered the publishing business, was one of color and adventure.

After he "graduated" as a printer's apprentice at Cobourg, Ontario, in 1849, the next 25 years were spent in moving from place to place much in the fashion of itinerant printers of the latter part of the 19th century.

At different times, he owned newspapers at Owen Sound and Windsor, Ontario and at Winnipeg, where he also worked as a printer with five different newspapers.

He never seemed to be far away from armed conflict or uprising. In 1866, he served in an army unit during a Fenian raid at Windsor, Ontario, and in 1871 with one at Pembina, Manitoba. One of the plants he worked in at Winnipeg was seized by insurgents and another was wrecked by a mob.

In 1869, on behalf of the Canadian faction in Winnipeg, he turned out a number of proclamations on a hand press. These disturbed the Métis leader, Louis Riel, in no uncertain way, causing Laurie to hasten across the border into the United States.

During the Riel rebellion, his plant at Battleford came through unscathed, though his letters show he made claims for furniture, books, crockery and other articles taken from his home by officers and members of the regiment stationed at Fort Battleford.

Quotations from his letters at that time revealed something of the man, and something of the troubled times in which he lived.

One reads: "Our N.W. Council is peculiarly constituted that it is in many ways anything but a representative institution. It has no money of its own save the pittance collected from offenders against the Ordinances, and is largely confined to carrying out the laws and regulations framed at Ottawa by those who know not whereof they speak when they try to legislate for us."

In 1880: "If you think well of it I will publish the enclosed advt.—you supplying electrotype (printing cut) of wire— for one year for eight dollars, payable next March, in wire."

Again: "Everything in the way of merchandise for this

country, is ordered season preceding its shipment—e.g., spring goods ordered in fall and vice versa."

"Allow me here to say that the pernicious dime novel always pictures the Indian scout as a cold-blooded fiend, revelling in deeds of gore. Our best men in that line are the quietest, most unostentatious and tender-hearted men in the country . . . they never come in from an expedition without bringing something for the sick in the hospital. It may be only a pocketful of eggs of wild fowl or some bird good for food."

And this treasure: "This Canada of ours is a large country and provides wide fields of labor for those who traverse the plains, as well as those who go down to the sea in ships, with the reward of at least an approving conscience for those who do well what their hands find to do."

Laurie's many writings and letters, now mainly in the archives of Saskatchewan, are accepted as accurate reflections of the background of local and territorial events, thus becoming a source of reference eagerly sought by research students.

AL MAZUR

While Al Mazur, as publisher of *The Hudson Bay Post-Review*, lives on the north-eastern frontier of Saskatchewan newspaperdom, he is known throughout the province as a dedicated promoter of the many resources of the area.

He is a strong supporter of worthwhile community projects, and his success in this field is well recognized. The powers that be in government circles open their doors to him and listen attentively to what he says. And his name is familiar to an exclusive group of sportsmen throughout Canada and in the northern and central portions of the United States.

His first community improvement activity, was to campaign personally and through his newspaper for a water and sewer system. This was followed by a drive for street paving. Both were eventually undertaken by the town when his sound reasoning eventually converted opponents.

His next promotion was a clean-up campaign. This he began (and ended successfully) with a two-page spread in

The Post-Review, carrying pictures of piles of garbage and untidy back lots within the town limits. Then he left town for two weeks.

He expected, when he returned, to be greeted with hostility, by some angry ratepayers whose unsightly properties had been pictured. He was more than agreeably surprised.

Almost all of the unsanitary accumulations had been cleaned up, and there were no unpleasant recriminations. The tell-tale pictures had generated shame rather than hostility.

But Al Mazur's chief claim to fame came through a clever project that made the Hudson Bay area famous from one end of the country to the other. The project was to entice more big game hunters to visit the area in the hunting season.

To begin with, he coined the pretentious sounding slogan: "Hudson Bay, the Moose Capital of the World."

These words caught the eye of sportsmen in far-away places in Canada. Most of them had fixed ideas about the superiority of their respective areas over all others with regard to size and numbers of the moose population.

Al, however, had been busy gathering statistics from here and there before he publicized the slogan. Hunters in both Ontario and Alberta challenged his claim, but when he quoted the results of his research he heard no more from them. The figures amply supported his claim.

He arranged a local competition known as The Moose Derby, in co-operation with the Saskatchewan Department of Natural Resources. Winners each year have their records scanned by the Saskatchewan Fish and Game League. The latter in turn record their trophy winners with the Boone and Crockett Club in the United States; that organization maintains the official fish and game trophy records for the continent. Already three moose heads from Hudson Bay have been entered in these continental records as top winners.

Mazur produces a special hunting issue of *The Post-Review*, a copy of which goes to every purchaser of a Saskatchewan deer or moose hunting license. Thus interest in the area is well sustained.

Records prove that each year well over 50 percent of the

moose harvest in Saskatchewan, is taken from Hudson Bay region.

Registrations for the annual Moose Derby are made at *The Post-Review* office, when each entrant is also enrolled in the "Royal Order of the Hanging Moose Hide" and receives a certificate, stating the holder is recognized as being a "Son of a Moose."

With the moose propaganda moving along steadily, Mazur began a second campaign promoting the sport of angling for whitefish and it would not be unexpected if one day he announced a second slogan emphasizing that the biggest whitefish in the world are caught in north-eastern Saskatchewan.

Just to waken up the provincial folk, in and close to government circles, who might have considered the sporting opportunities of the northern woods, lakes and streams as being too remote from civilization to be worth promoting, Mazur in 1964, when he was first vice-president of the Saskatchewan Division, CWNA, invited Premier Lloyd and his cabinet and a few others to a dinner.

The piece de resistance of the dinner was mooseburgers followed by Mazur's tastefully spiced story of Hudson Bay, the moose capital of the world, past, present and future.

The next year, when he was president of the newspaper association, he repeated his hospitality to the same group. On this occasion he featured smoked whitefish prepared in Hudson Bay style. His remarks on that occasion concerned the advantages to the province in promoting in every possible way, a greater sale and consumption of whitefish on continental markets as well as attracting greater numbers of tourist fishermen to the province.

Al Mazur is widely known as an innovator in the industry. He was the first weekly publisher in the province to install offset equipment. While the new method of printing was still limited to large commercial city plants, he saw its advantages and benefits for a country weekly operation.

As a pioneer user of this modern method of putting words and pictures on paper, he became a source of valuable assistance to other publishers contemplating a similar investment.

The *Hudson Bay Post-Review* is an outstanding example of fine offset newspaper production, and as such is a consistent prize-winner in annual competition in its circulation class.

CAMERON R. McINTOSH

Cameron Ross McIntosh can best be described in but a few words. Throughout his long lifetime, he has been an "intense Canadian."

From his 'teen-age years, his burning objective has been to create within the hearts of all Canadians a deep-rooted patriotism and loyalty to the country of their birth or adoption, and to inspire in them the same vision as he held of a great future for Canada.

In a sense, his greatest contribution in this regard came after he moved to Saskatchewan. His newspaper editorials stimulated a new interest in, and knowledge of, the "north country." And his strong sense of patriotism was evident in many of his speeches as a member of parliament.

Early in his boyhood days, he developed a theory that the basic need of a young and growing nation was that the intellect of youth should be so guided as to produce men and women of high moral principle with a self-reliant, broad, wholesome outlook. Such attitudes, he reasoned, would ensure the best possible social environment, to the everlasting benefit of the nation.

It was natural that school teaching first appealed to him as an opportunity whereby he could contribute to the promotion of his ideals. First teaching in rural schools, he observed the great need of having pupils develop the ability to express themselves clearly, in social contacts or from the public platform.

He developed a type of inter-class discussion which, after the passing of years, is now being seriously considered as a worthwhile extension of the curriculum. The main difference is in the degree of application.

Mr. McIntosh used his program only with high school pupils who were well on the way to the establishment of firm convictions, with well-formed ideas—and ideals.

His classes became discussion periods of many topics. Statements, questions and answers revealed that the students' minds were far more active than one might have supposed.

It was only a step from there to take up the study and practice of public speaking. This was while he was teaching at Athens, Ontario, at the Public and Model School, after having served seven years in rural schools.

On the inspector's first visit he was surprised to see the methods used by Mr. McIntosh, but considered it to be a "stunt" which would soon fade out. On his second visit, he saw that the teacher was not only carrying on with his unusual technique, he was also getting outstanding results, and the Athens school led all other similar institutions in the province.

So Cameron McIntosh went on the record as the first in Canada to teach public speaking in schools.

After serving at Athens for six years, he was appointed principal of Perth, Ontario, Public and Model School where he continued his successful career.

It was here he first took an active part in politics, when he campaigned on behalf of a Liberal candidate during an election. Some members of the school board became incensed at this, but the Meighen family, whose cousin, Arthur Meighen, later became prime minister of Canada, defended the right of any board employee to take political action. Cries for his resignation were heard no more. Mr. McIntosh, at times, with a bit of a twinkle in his eye, will allow "there are some good Conservatives."

Relatives in Saskatchewan added their influence to the call of the west. He moved to North Battleford, Saskatchewan in 1911, to become principal of the North Battleford Public School, which took in grades I to XII.

In his new position, he again encountered criticism for taking an active interest in the Liberal party, resulting in the filing of his resignation, but just previous to doing so, he purchased the town's only newspaper, *The News*. The day his resignation took effect, he became the newspaper's editor and publisher.

An interesting sidelight was the fact that in the fall of 1912, he was elected a trustee of the North Battleford School Board, defeating one of the men who the previous spring had taken exception to his political activity.

Following his arrival in North Battleford, it did not take long for the observant and forward-looking Cameron McIntosh to appreciate the great potential of the north. He became "the man of vision" regarding its resources and development.

He was years ahead of others in recognizing the possibilities which would eventually grow into realities by adding population, industry and wealth to an area that to many appeared far away and barren of resources other than scrub pine forest and the indigenous wild life.

Today, the development of mineral, timber, fur, fishing and tourist resources, together with the surge of prospecting parties across vast spaces of the northland, confirm the foresight so often evident in McIntosh's prophecies.

It was in the early 1920s that he took his first step to publicise the north country and its little known resources.

Covering different areas of territory each year, he published special "development issues" of his newspaper, filling its columns with descriptions of commercial, industrial, resort and other opportunities which he came across in his travels over hundreds of miles of territory. These issues contained up to 50 pages each, a size never before approached by any western weekly newspaper. Altogether, they were a compelling factor in increasing population, rural and urban, and in the resulting business expansion.

His personal coverage of the territory brought many friends. In 1925, he was urged to run as a Liberal candidate in the federal election. This he won by a substantial majority, and was re-elected in 1926, 1930 and 1935, serving as Member of Parliament until the election of 1940.

It had been Mr. McIntosh's privilege to see some of his visions materialize such as the Hudson Bay Railway projected by the "On-to-the-Bay Association," in which he took a leading part.

Following his election to Parliament in 1925, his forceful arguments from the floor of the House, were a vital factor in the government's final decision to have the line built to Churchill from the point where it had been stalled by the impact of First World War. Actually, there had been a time when it appeared almost certain that the project would be forgotten.

His vast knowledge of the terrain of the north country and of the coastal characteristics of Hudson's Bay played a vital part in influencing the decision to make Churchill the terminus of the railway rather than Nelson.

One biographer stated: "Cameron McIntosh, at that time a handsome, well set up figure, of a mature mind and with a profound knowledge of politics and government, took an active and increasingly important part in the work of the house. He was listened to with respect by his colleagues in the caucus and in the discussion which arose out of the ever-changing crisis in the party. (The Liberal government was a minority at the time.) When he addressed the house he at once attracted attention and respect. He was already a trained orator who knew how to marshall his facts and to express them eloquently and forcibly."

During his 15 years in Parliament he repeatedly introduced a resolution leading to the adoption of a distinctive Canadian flag. While his efforts did not immediately result in such action being taken by any government, there is little doubt but his continuing plea had much to do with the now familiar maple leaf flag, introduced in 1967.

Seventy-five miles north of North Battleford, is a village named Dorintosh.

Mr. McIntosh tells the story of the origin of the name. He had been advised that he was to be honored by having a town named after him, but being with true Scottish sentimentality, he suggested that the first syllable of the name of his birthplace, Dornoch, Ontario, be used in the composite word of Dorintosh. His wish was acted upon.

Ever active in local promotions, Mr. McIntosh founded the North-western Broadcasting Company, original owners of radio station CJNB, and served as company president for five years.

He was a pioneer director of what is now the Hudson Bay Route Association and is today an honorary director. This organization aimed at the expansion of trade between Canada and overseas nations through the port of Churchill.

He used his newspaper as well as his own voice in organizing a Canadian Club in North Battleford following the First World War, with its main activity, the financing of the local cenotaph.

His was a Presbyterian heritage, with the uncompromising qualities of the Scottish Covenanters. For him life carried serious responsibilities. As a result of his presence at the General Assemblies of his church, his strong personality and vigorous utterances were known and remembered throughout church circles from coast to coast.

He continued to urge the construction of a Northern Trans-Canada highway and along with others who had long seen the need for the alternate route, saw the Yellowhead highway become a reality in 1969.

In 1959, he was recognized by the Canadian Weekly Newspapers Association when it conferred on him an honorary life membership.

Mr. McIntosh was always an ardent champion of Sir Wilfrid Laurier, to whom he bears a striking physical resemblance. Both had white hair; both had a distinguished bearing with facial features very much alike.

Of this Mr. McIntosh was well aware, and for years kept wearing the same straight, high, white collar and style of tie in the Laurier tradition, long after the fashion had changed. When referred to as the "Laurier of the North" he always felt honored.

Since his involvement in the newspaper business through the purchase of *The News* in 1912, he has helped bring about many changes in the local field.

In 1925, because his duties as a member of parliament removed him a great deal of the time from the local scene, he organized a company named the North Battleford News Limited, in which he was the main stock holder.

This company acquired the historic newspaper, *The Press* of Battleford in 1949, and in 1953 also purchased the opposition newspaper, *The North Battleford Optimist* which had operated since 1912.

In 1959 *The St. Walburg Enterprise* and *Paradise Hill Beacon* were bought, followed by the *Cut Knife Highway* 40 *Courier* in 1960.

For some years *The News-Optimist* has been issued as a semi-weekly with a second newspaper, *The Cut Knife Courier* being produced weekly from the same plant.

It was in 1951 that Mr. McIntosh appointed his son Irwin as editor, adding the position of general manager to this role in 1952.

On July 7, 1969, Cameron Ross McIntosh celebrated his 98th birthday in his beautiful ranch style home on the north bank of the North Saskatchewan river with an enchanting view of the wide valley. His wife, Pearle Susanne, had passed away in 1968. She too was a talented woman, taking an active interest in many important social issues of her time.

Their years together had been years of happiness, for they were a devoted couple, creating a house filled with warmth, good cheer and a stimulating atmosphere.

In his quiet moments, Mr. McIntosh must reflect with much satisfaction as the results of one of his many achievements—his poems. In 1966 a book containing over 500 of these was published; most of them had been composed since 1940. He is currently working on a new volume of poems to be titled "Canada at the Crossroads, Nationally and Internationally."

One need only read a few of these to catch the theme of the author's ambition in life—to stir in the hearts of Canadians a deeper appreciation of their country. His own deep love of Canada can be sensed in the lines of *"Our Own Dominion Land."*

"Vast Northland by three oceans bound,
And mountains, plains and waters deep.
As round the earth thy deeds resound
Thou hast an honoured name to keep!
At home and o'er the seas far flung,
The pillars prized of nationhood

217

We must build deep, to lift aloft
An approved bilingual statehood
That can the future clear
And strive for things Divine that stand
The tests of peace and threats of hate
In our own blest Dominion land.
Dear land! Lead on as ages roll,
That freedom we shall have of soul."

JOHN SCOTT

Away back in late 1899, an old lady fortune-teller in the little town of Chelsea, Ontario, told John Scott, then a lad of 17 years, that he would be going on a long journey and would be in business for himself within a year.

He just laughed, considering it a bit of nonsense, even though the 25 cent fee paid the lady might well have been considered a waste to be deplored at a time when money was real money.

John had just finished an apprenticeship in the printing trade, during the course of which he had been paid $20 for the first year, $40 for the second and $60 for the third. His work often started at 6 a.m. and night hours were frequent. And in spite of his scepticism, the fortune-teller's forecast came true.

By November 1, 1900 he had purchased *The Whitewood Herald,* at Whitewood, Saskatchewan. He had come west to help his brother-in-law, Ernie Zingg, establish *The Post* at Wapella.

The purchase of *The Herald* included very little in the way of plant. The office building had a roof but no ceiling.

From a two-page homeprint and two-page ready print paper, five-column size, he soon had it built up to a six-column, Four-page home print, four-page ready print paper.

The type was all hand set at first and for a time he was manager, editor, reporter and printer. The only help he engaged was an old man who would come in on press day to run the big ink roller over the newspaper type forms on the hand operated old style press.

Soon John had a linotype, power press and all the rest of a good plant and a good building in which it was housed.

Today John Scott is 94 years old.

Little did he think after coming west that he would spend all his life in Whitewood or that he would create a record in the weekly newspaper field in Saskatchewan. No other person has been sole owner and publisher of the only weekly in one town for anywhere near the number of years that he guided *The Whitewood Herald* continuously through economic ups and downs. Scott's score in this respect was 55 years.

If anyone should get the idea from this record of "immo-bility", so opposite to the usual western pattern, that John was quite content to let the world pass his door, and lag behind in the march of modern progress, such a thought should be discarded immediately and completely.

His newspaper was always foward-looking and well edited, and his news stories a paragon of accuracy. His business was carried on with precision. He was never a recluse in any sense, though he made full use of his own fine library at every opportunity. He assumed his share of community responsibility and had a smile for everyone.

He served as president of the Saskatchewan Weekly Newspapers Association in 1933 with distinction.

WILLIAM JOHN REDMOND

When a young man from Peterborough, Ontario, eager to experience the glamour and excitement of far away places and events arrived in Maple Creek, Saskatchewan, in 1899, with its wide-open spaces of big ranches, unpredictable cowboys, Indians, law-breakers from across the border, western hospit-ality and good people of the pioneer cowtown, he found the Utopia he was seeking.

William John Redmond, traveller, policeman, publisher and raconteur loved every minute of it. With the passing years, he became an intriguing example of the old western breed of men with loyalty to the area's traditions to which he himself contributed so much.

Even in his retirement, the attractions of other places and

climates never tempted him to leave the countryside he knew so well and the warm friends who meant so much to him.

He first went to Maple Creek wearing the scarlet uniform of the North West Mounted Police, with which he had just enlisted. His regimental number was 3418, which reveals that he was a member of the force during its most colorful period, and at a time when it first fulfilled the purpose for which it was created—the maintenance of law and order on the wide open spaces of the western plains. He retired from the force in 1908 with the rank of sergeant.

In 1909, he purchased *The Maple Creek News* which provided scope for his writing talent. With the introduction of his column "Ragson Tatters" his writings were widely quoted. He published *The News* for 45 years, selling out to Walter Migowski in 1955.

In 1902, he was one of 24 men selected to represent the NWMP at the coronation of King Edward VII in London, England.

He served as mayor of Maple Creek for a total of 10 years, first in 1914-15-16 and then in 1920-21, and so successfully that when the difficult depression years of the thirties arrived, the citizens again conscripted his talent for the years 1931-35.

Many were the times that his opinion on administrative problems was sought by government departments and officials, including premiers, as his private papers later revealed.

No other brief sentence could be quite as revealing of his inward emotions as the one he once uttered: "I came west to kill Indians but got to love them."

For John Redmond was everybody's friend. To those suffering or in need he was always sympathetic, without regard for race, creed, color, or social standing. This was characteristic of his whole philosophy of life.

One of his particular friends was a laborer who lived in a shack "across the tracks" with only a big mongrel dog for company. He had a habit of imbibing much too freely at times, which further isolated him from human companionship. Yet there was something in this man's background which appealed to John Redmond. So much so that, following his sudden demise one night, John insisted that there was be to no pauper's funeral but a church service and a decent burial. Marking the grave is a marble slab taken from an old pool table and set in cement. Its inscription ends with the words "Good Old Sam." The engraver of the lettering is unknown, the secret known only to John Redmond.

He enjoyed every minute of living, and had a great sense of humor, and a feel for drama in everyday situations. His "Ragson Tatters" column became widely recognized as top-flight material, each with its generous serving of cowtown humor and homespun philosophy.

Here, in his own inimitable style, is the column that told how he happened to come west:

"Having crossed the Atlantic a couple of times as nurse-maid to cattle and sheep, I was filled with wanderlust and decided to seek adventure with the North West Mounted Police. The cost of a colonist ticket to Regina was $27.50. I had $35 . . . So I hit on the bright idea of making the Grand Trunk carry me as far as North Bay and the dear old Canadian Pacific from there to Regina as a non-paying passenger. Slipping off the blind one morning, side away from the station of course, I watched the darndest bunch of people I ever clapped my eyes on getting out of the colonist cars behind. On arriving at Winnipeg I bought a copy of the *Free Press* and learned I had entered the west with Clifford Sifton's first importation of Doukhobors. When I spotted them north of Lake Superior, little did I think they would make a bigger noise in the west than I ever would. Still, if I would strip naked, walk down the main stem from my office, drop a bomb on the CPR tracks, I would probably make at least a 36-point heading clear across Canada, and of a certainty, no probability, be escorted to the hoosegow by a courteous member of the RCMP."

On reaching Regina he "footed" it out to the police barracks to enlist and this experience he recorded as follows:

"Asked my age by the captain, I gave it as 22 (the minimum for enlisting) although I was only a few days over 20. Looking backward in the years that followed I was appalled at the glib manner in which I lied. As a matter of fact I never

recovered from the habit, harmless lies of course, until I returned to my first love—newspaperwork—where misrepresentation
of any kind is simply not tolerated. Following a once-over,
he shook his head and intimated I was too slight. Don't blame
him any; I hadn't been eating regularly and was down to 136
pounds. Visions of going back down town to grab a job on
The Regina Leader loomed before my eyes, and I all set to
kill Indians! However, Dr. Bell, the police surgeon, knew top
physical quality when it came under his observation. Fortunately, in those years they didn't look too closely into mental
fitness. Had they done so my extreme modesty might have
been mistaken for stupidity, and the force would have lost
what was soon to become one of its shining ornaments."

This last sly reference had to do with the honor coming to
him three years later when he became one of 24 Mounted
Police chosen out of the entire force to attend the coronation
of King Edward VII.

One can picture the members of the NWMP group taking
part in all the pomp and ceremony of that event and exhibiting
the results of weeks of precision drill, looking neither to the
right nor left. Their stern and immobile faces would indicate
they were only concerned as to how perfectly they could carry
out the part allotted to them. Yet among them were minds
quick to respond to the unusual. Redmond wrote:

"I was amused to hear the crowds when the Mounted
Police hove in sight, telling one another, 'here come the
Indian fighters.' Indian fighters! Phooey! I joined the force
to kill Indians and ended up liking them, and to a certain
extent understanding them. Corporal Fitzgerald was riding
on my left. He whispered to me that the crowd had the adjective
all right but the noun all wrong. Even yet I am prepared to
go to the mat with any person who feels like tramping on the
original owners of this country."

The unruffled and philosophical manner in which Redmond accepted unpleasant situations is evident in the following
quotation from his column:

"Within a couple of weeks of my arrival (at Maple Creek)
I was ordered to the Ten-Mile Detachment. The first job that
Sergeant Bottley put me at was digging postholes and cutting

down trees for posts to make a fence around the old Fort Walsh cemetery (in the Cypress Hills). As I sat to rest frequently (never did think much of hard work) I got thinking of how cruel fate could be. For eight years the remains of men lying there had rested well in a fenceless cemetery while several hundred able-bodied men had loafed the time away just a few hundred yards distant. Why couldn't they have erected the fence instead of letting the job lie to be pushed off on me . . . ? Gazing at the blisters on my hands it struck me that a cemetery seemed an appropriate place to inter all the romantic notions I had cherished during my 'teen-age years. A few weeks later, looking through the official detachment diary, I noticed that Sergeant Bottley and I had proceeded daily to the site of the cemetery to build the fence. As Bottley had no part of it I was a bit peeved, but a few months on the force had taught me to keep my trap shut when talking book to those who outranked me."

Redmond had a rare personality which left a lasting impression on anyone meeting him for the first time.

One example of this: Ten years after he had been a patient at Mayo Clinic, at Rochester, Minnesota, one of its doctors, while on a holiday trip happened by chance to meet Redmond's daughter-in-law. He immediately asked if she was related to a patient by the same name from Canada. The doctor remembered his conversations with Redmond, long after contacts with hundreds of others had been forgotten.

William John Redmond passed away in hospital at Maple Creek, September 16, 1957. At his funeral, six scarlet-coated members of the RCMP were pall-bearers. Among the eight honorary pall-bearers were Colonel S. T. Wood, former Commissioner of the force, whose presence indicated the respect in which the policeman turned newspaperman was held.

Redmond's uniform, badges, buttons, medal and New Testament with the signatures of the 24 men attending the coronation are in the RCMP museum in Regina.

William John Redmond made an important contribution to the weekly newspaper profession in Saskatchewan, and to the historical records of Maple Creek and the surrounding ranching country.

223

SAMUEL NATHAN WYNN, LL.D.

It was in 1904 that Sam Wynn arrived in Yorkton, Saskatchewan, to take a position as monoline operator with *The Enterprise*.

Records substantiate the claim that he has been engaged in the weekly newspaper business in Saskatchewan, if not in all of Canada, for the greatest number of years of any editor or publisher. Though he sold the Enterprise Publishing Company to Thomson Newspapers Limited in 1963, he remained as its publisher, and continues to write his own long established front page column on current events in his usual crisp style.

He established residence in Yorkton at a time when there were only a few newspapers in the North West Territories, and at a time when weekly newspaper plants operated with the barest minimum of necessary equipment.

Common to most printing shops were uncomfortable working conditions, shortage of qualified help, long working hours and financial problems.

Sam had been receiving $9 per week to operate a monoline type setting machine in Toronto. It was natural that $18 per week offered by *The Yorkton Enterprise* was sufficient to entice him to that little western town. Actually, he had received equally good offers from Medicine Hat and Moose Jaw, but the Doukhobor people had settled near Yorkton, and his enquiring mind led him to make the choice he did, so that he could learn at first hand what these new immigrants were like.

The Enterprise plant was located in a disused church building. Its bare rafters exposed a vast area of overhead space which, during sub zero weather, defied all efforts to get the shop warm enough to work in by mid-day, even with a small degree of comfort.

On one occasion, an imposing stone (marble) about four feet in width was so cold that when some hot water was accidentally spilled on its surface, it cracked from side to side.

The owner of the building decided to improve things by raising the church frame structure and enclosing the ground floor with concrete walls for the printing office and plant.

This project did little towards providing a more congenial

workshop. The few small windows permitted only a little daylight to enter from the outside and the overhead space became a public hall where public meetings and dances were held.

The dancers, too, had their unpleasant time, when the newspaper staff worked overtime with coal oil lamps for illumination. The continuous chug-chug of the gasoline engine and the vibrations of the floor from the revolving shaft were not synchronized with the rhythm of the orchestra: the two "beats" were confusing.

Sam recalls that the one-cylinder gasoline engine was considered a marvellous creation but not then familiar to many people as regards its operation. During one cold spell it just refused to start. An "expert" was called in and after he had taken it apart and reassembled it, it still refused to fulfill its duty. It was taken apart a second time, reassembled, but with the same result.

Sam came up with an idea. By going outside and knocking off the accumulation of ice at the top of the exhaust pipe he had the engine running in a few minutes. From then on he always first looked askance at anyone labelled "expert".

The following year E. B. McKay, editor and manager, resigned and Mr. Wynn accepted the dual position at a salary of $25 per week.

With the help of two apprentices Sam Wynn began what was to be a long and illustrous career. His own newly-assumed duties included editorial writing, news reporting, advertising solicitation, commercial printing sales and office management.

The Enterprise had been operating in the red, (which was not uncommon in the early days of weekly newspapers on the prairies) but from the time Sam took over, the business prospered.

The Enterprise began publication as a small venture in 1896 in a sparsely equipped little office. From then until 1904, when *The Enterprise Publishing Co. Ltd.* was formed, it had four different editors.

Three prominant Conservatives, with political ambitions, purchased the plant and installed considerable modern equipment in a larger building, the aforementioned disused church.

With Liberal governments in power provincially and federally, local Liberals were incensed at the political power exercised by *The Enterprise*, and ten of them, mostly office-holders, put up $10,000 and established an opposition paper, *The Press*, in 1908, with R. W. Tuckwell as editor. In 1915, when Tuckwell moved to Lloydminster to found a weekly newspaper, another group took over and changed the name to *The Yorkton Times*. Unable to compete successfully with *The Enterprise*, *The Times* ceased publication in 1924. From then on, Yorkton was a one-paper town. Eschewing politics for independence, *The Enterprise* became a community newspaper in the best sense of the word.

Referring to those years, Mr. Wynn states: "While building *The Enterprise* up from nothing, eliminating competitors in both the weekly field and throw-away advertising sheets, I was too busy to look after my own interests."

Though the shareholders of *The Enterprise Publishing Co.* were reluctant to sell him shares at any time, he managed to pick up a few and finally acquired a 50 percent interest in a somewhat unusual fashion.

Requiring larger premises to take care of a growing business, the company proceeded with the erection of a new building. It is the one still occupied by *The Enterprise* and incidentally was the second one built under Mr. Wynn's management.

Before the building was completed, the company ran out of money. It was a made-to-order situation for him. By hocking his life insurance and borrowing to the limit he was able to gain a half interest, which, with his management role, gave him control of the company.

In 1922, under pressure from local merchants, *The Enterprise* became a semi-weekly. The production of any semi-weekly newspaper has problems not commonly understood, mainly as a result of one issue in each week having a sparse amount of advertising while the second issue bulges with it. This creates an uneven load of work for the printing staff. But in spite of this *The Enterprise* continued to overcome the handicap until the second of the depression years.

One week there was not a single display advertisement for

the Tuesday issue. Mr. Wynn decided not to produce it. In the Friday issue there was an announcement stating that due to a breakdown on the printing press, it had been impossible to print the Tuesday issue. From then on, *The Enterprise* continued as a weekly.

In 1963, Thomson Newspapers Ltd., owners of many daily and weekly newspapers in Canada, Great Britain and the United States negotiated with Mr. Wynn for the purchase of the business and completed the deal that year. He remained with them as publisher.

One of the annual projects instituted by Mr. Wynn was the newspaper's Empty Stocking Fund. This provided Christmas hampers for the needy, and each year the amount of money raised reached a substantial figure, requiring much time and effort in administration. A total of some $50,000 or more was collected throughout the years in appeals in the columns of *The Enterprise.*

Management of the fund, in co-operation with the Yorkton Benevolent Society, was assumed by the late Ken Mayhew, who had joined the staff as reporter, and rose to the position of editor. In recognition of his long and efficient service, the Rotary Club carried on the work under the name, The Kenny Mayhew Christmas Fund.

Through Mr. Wynn's management, *The Yorkton Enter-prise* became one of the top weekly newspapers in Canada, both as to circulation total and quality of content. It has taken many first prizes in national competitions over a long period of years, and while Sam Wynn always gave his staff full credit for their part in these triumphs, his own sure judgement was evident in every phase of the newspaper's operation.

Mr. Wynn has been active in many areas of public service. One can only wonder how he could ever find the time to do so many things—and do them all well.

He has been a director of the Yorkton Agricultural Society for 40 years, president of the Yorkton Rotary Club, president of the Yorkton Board of Trade, chairman of Board of Directors of Yorkton Union Hospital, president of the Saskatchewan Hospital Association.

Offices filled in provincial organizations include: trustee

of the Saskatchewan Anti-Tuberculosis League for many years; member of the Advisory Committee of Health Services Planning Commission, and president of the Saskatchewan Division Canadian Weekly Newspapers Association.

It was this association that honored him with the title of "Weekly Editor of Canada" when he completed 50 years of newspaper work. He is the only one ever to receive this title. The same group awarded him an honorary life membership in 1959.

So often, a home-towner's achievements are not given proper recognition. This is not the case with Sam Wynn.

He is an honorary member and past-president of the Yorkton Rotary Club, an honorary member of General Ross Branch, Royal Canadian Legion, honorary member of the Yorkton Agricultural Association and honorary member of the Yorkton Lions Club in recognition of 60 years of service to the community.

It was most fitting that in 1955, the honorary degree of Doctor of Laws was conferred on him by the University of Saskatchewan in recognition of his contribution to Canadian journalism.

The long record of service rendered over the years by Mr. Wynn has won the admiration, not only of his fellow newspapermen, but of people in all walks of life.

ALEXANDER KENNETH THOM

While A. K. Thom, publisher and editor of *The Wadena Herald*, Saskatchewan's first weekly newspaper, was not widely known within the fraternity, his story is one of unusual interest.

Though physical and economic difficulties were endured by many western pioneer publishers, few, if any, were so hard hit as was Thom. But in the face of much personal tribulation, he willingly gave of his time and energy to public life, resolving many problems of local concern.

He never accumulated much wealth, yet never complained when more than the average man's share of hardship weighed him down. He was the kind of personality that enriched all the communities in which he lived at various times.

Certainly, it was not his physical size which impressed, for Thom was small and frail, weighing about 120 pounds. Seeking to regain his health, he came from Ontario to Manitoba in 1898 on the advice of his physician, who had bluntly told him to move to the wide open spaces of the west if he wished to live.

He engaged in farm work near Morden, Manitoba, and gradually regained normal strength, together with a reserve of energy of which later stood him in good stead.

Because of his physical background, it is not to be wondered that he spent much of his lifetime in outdoor activities, rather than in the confines of a newspaper office.

Beginning in 1901, he worked at *The Yorkton Enterprise* for almost a year. Then seeking the invigorating influence of sunshine and prairie breeze in 1902, his wife and he built a cabin on farm land a short distance south of the present site of Quill Lake.

When the Canadian National Railway line was under construction through the area a few years later, he contracted to move supplies from Yorkton to Quill Lake to add to his meagre farm income. This was no child's play. There were no graded roads, but only rutted prairie trails that twisted hither and thither between the dense bush and the sloughs.

It was necessary to ford streams in flood, always with the chance of disaster. On one occasion, one of his horses got its head down and entangled in the harness while crossing a swift running creek. He plunged into the water, pulled its head up and began to readjust the harness, when he was knocked unconscious by the frightened horse's struggles. When he came to, he was lying safely on the bank. By good fortune, he had hung on to the harness and been dragged out to land by his team.

During the rush of American settlers into the area, great confusion resulted from the failure of the land company from which they had purchased the land, to properly organize the mass migration. Records were contradictory and some found that the parcels of land they had supposedly purchased were claimed by others.

The government engaged Mr. Thom to straighten out the mess—a task he completed with much satisfaction to all involved.

It was in 1908 that Thom moved to Wadena and founded *The Herald* which was enthusiastically received. The very first copy printed was put up for auction and sold for $15.

In common with all early prairie newspaper plants, the first equipment was rather primitive. All the type was set by hand, but this did not deter Thom from turning out a well edited paper. Eventually a linotype and other pieces of modern equipment were added.

When the First World War broke out, Thom enlisted in the 214th Battalion and rose to the rank of captain. He was quartermaster for the unit. Following the war he returned to *The Herald*.

Later, he was elected mayor of Wadena. Evidence of his good administration remain in well engineered streets bordered with trees.

Failing health finally forced him to sell *The Herald*. He then bought land amid spruce forest near Stony Lake, and later was elected reeve of the municipality in which he resided.

The nature of the man would not allow idleness. There were times when he was 60 years of age, that he hauled fence posts 40 miles through the bush.

He had no fear of snow and severe cold when caught by night away from home. He had found that a comfortable sleep could be had by choosing good tree shelter, shovelling snow to bare a sandy spot on which a fire could be built to warm the ground, then scattering the fire and laying a mattress of spruce boughs on the warm sand. For anyone well wrapped in blankets, this made a warm bed for the night.

One of the severest ordeals suffered by the Thom family, was a tragedy which took the lives of Mrs. Thom's mother, sister and brother-in-law. The Thoms took a four-year-old nephew who survived and raised him as their own son.

When Thom was 65, Dame Fortune dealt him a severe

financial blow with the destruction of his farm home and other buildings. In the opinion of his many friends, this disaster had one redeeming feature, and that was to induce him to give up farming, a job which he no longer had the strength to pursue. He sold his farm, and with Mrs. Thom retired in Wadena where they adjusted slowly to a less active life.

Their final years ended in happier vein. Their 50th wedding anniversary was joyfully celebrated with hosts of friends participating.

Then in the spring of 1954, they departed this life as they would have wished. They died within three weeks of each other when they were both over 80 years of age, leaving with their many friends, memories of a life of triumph over a multitude of adversities.

APPENDIX

PRESIDENTS OF
SASKATCHEWAN WEEKLY NEWSPAPERS
ASSOCIATIONS

1918–1919—Cameron R. McIntosh, North Battleford
1919–1920—Cameron R. McIntosh, North Battleford
1920–1921—T. M. Marshall, Weyburn
1921–1922—S. N. Wynn, Yorkton
1922–1923—S. N. Wynn, Yorkton
1923–1924—S. N. Wynn, Yorkton
1924–1925—Jas. McDonald, Unity
1925–1926—E. Garrett, Watrous
1926–1927—E. Garrett, Watrous
1927–1928—T. H. B. McCullough, Weyburn
1928–1929—S. R. Moore, Swift Current
1929–1930—H. G. Sheldrake, North Battleford
1930–1931—Walter Ashfield, Grenfell
1931–1932—Andrew King, Rouleau
1932–1933—John Scott, Whitewood
1933–1934—Donald C. Dunbar, Estevan
1934–1935—Harold Gamble, Gull Lake
1935–1936—E. S. Zingg, Wapella
1936–1937—William T. Morphy, Viscount
1937–1938—C. W. Holmes, Rosetown
1938–1939—James Greenblat, Swift Current
1939–1940—John A. Vopni, Davidson
1940–1941—Fred Whisken, Punnichy
1941–1942—W. C. Needham, Wynyard
1942–1943—William Young, Saltcoats
1943–1944—J. A. McGowan, Watrous
1944–1945—Robert Moore, Swift Current
1945–1946—W. E. Sharp, Shaunavon

1946–1947—Ernest G. Quick, Weyburn
1947–1948—S. J. Dornan, LL.D., Alameda
1948–1949—T. E. Scriver, Wolseley
1949–1950—Gerald Humphrey, Nokomis
1950–1951—George Lancaster, Melfort
1951–1952—Stirling King, Estevan
1952–1953—Sydney Stevens, Shaunavon
1953–1954—Ken Mayhew, Yorkton
1954–1955—John Pinckney, Rosetown
1955–1956—Walter Telfer, Humboldt
1956–1957—G. M. McKay, Moosomin
1957–1958—Irwin McIntosh, North Battleford
1958–1959—Ken Millar, Semans
1959–1960—Walter Migowsky, Maple Creek
1960–1961—J. C. Adair, Eatonia
1961–1962—R. S. Reid, Kindersley
1962–1963—W. B. Needham, Wynyard
1963–1964—Al Mazur, Hudson Bay
1964–1965—H. S. Scriver, Wolseley
1965–1966—Ernie Neufeld, Weyburn
1966–1967—John Ives, Tisdale
1967–1968—Joseph Ashfield, Whitewood
1968–1969—W. Morphy, Biggar
1969–1970—R. C. Squires, Wadena.

Honorary Life Members of
Saskatchewan Weekly Newspapers Association

Dr. S. J. Dornan, LL.D.   Robert Moore
Andrew King   Dave Belbeck
James Greenblat   Dr. S. N. Wynn, LL.D.
John Scott   Cameron R. McIntosh
E. G. Quick

Saskatchewan Honorary Life Members of
Canadian Weekly Newspapers Association

Dr. S. J. Dornan, LL.D.   Cameron R. McIntosh
Walter Ashfield   E. G. Quick
John A. Vopni   Robert Moore
Dr. S. N. Wynn, LL.D.   William Telfer
Andrew King